THE
PRESCRIPTION
FOR
Overcoming

Your Remedy to Fulfilling your Divine
Purpose and Living the Life of Your Dreams

ANNETTA ALEXANDER, MD, MPH

Purpose Publishing
13194 US Highway 301 S #417
Riverview, FL 33578
http://www.PurposePublishing.com

Dedication

To my incredible mother, thank you for raising me to believe in myself and know that I can accomplish anything I set my mind to. You gave me the most incredible gifts: faith, compassion, love, humility, and confidence. During one of my most difficult moments of wanting to give up on my dream, you told me I was not a quitter, which meant everything to me. Thank you for never doubting or questioning my life choices. Thank you for reminding me at every stage of my journey that I needed to write this book. Although your memory fades, may you always know in your heart that you are loved and the best mother I could have ever had.

Contents

Acknowledgments vii

Introduction ix

Chapter One : Know Thyself 1

Chapter Two : Know Your Worth 11

Chapter Three : Eat NO for Breakfast 19

Chapter Four : You are Not a Quitter 31

Chapter Five : Believe in Yourself 39

Chapter Six : Step Out of Your Comfort Zone 49

Chapter Seven : Stepping Into Your Comfort Zone 67

Chapter Eight : Keep Moving 77

Chapter Nine : Positive on Purpose 87

Chapter Ten : Dare to Dream 97

Endnotes 111

About The Author 121

Acknowledgments

To God be the glory. I owe everything to God and I am grateful for his grace and mercy.

To my sister, Belinda, thank you for always being so brave and outspoken, always supporting me, and being the "natural" healer of the family.

To my little sister, Desma, thank you for your support, for always being there for me when I needed it, and for the many times you stepped up as the big sister.

To my sister, Mary, thank you for always being a listening ear and making every conversation with you so pleasantly beautiful as you are.

To my father, Blaise, thank you for instilling in me that handwork definitely pays off and for being the best father to me. You have taught me the importance of being happy and that going to sleep with a smile on my face is everything.

To my cousin-sister, Brenda, we bonded later in life, but it felt like we were always so close and bonded at the navel strings. I am grateful for every moment and experience we shared and will cherish them forever.

To my sister from another mother, Paula, you could probably write this book because you know me so well. Thank you always for your support. Our foundation and the life experiences we shared throughout the years created a strong bond that distance could never sever.

To all my family and friends who have cheered me on along the way, I love you all.

To my husband, Peter, you are undoubtedly the most amazing and wonderful person I have ever met. To my husband, who always supports my dreams and ideas and makes me feel larger than life itself—BIG. Thank you for your constant support in all my endeavors and for inspiring me to add pediatrics to internal medicine. Most importantly, thank you for always believing in me. Each year, our lives get more exciting, and I can't wait to see where our journey will take us. I love you with all my heart.

To my patients whom I serve and who have inspired me, I wish you divine health and happiness.

Introduction

My mother has always been so impressed with my life goal that she mentioned it to one of my high school teachers, who exclaimed, "She is finally doing what she always wanted to do!"

"Wow! Did I always want to be a doctor?" I wondered. Someone out there knew that I expressed my desire to be a doctor. Unfortunately, I did not remember expressing this previously, at least not in high school. Yet somehow, my teacher remembered that it was my dream to be a doctor.

What happened? How did I get lost along the way? How did I forget my dream? How did it come back to me? These are some of the questions I pondered throughout the years as I reflected on my life.

More than fifteen years after starting medical school, I am privileged to share my experiences and the lessons I've learned along the way. I'm also happy to report that I have gotten the answers to my questions and will share with you how to avoid straying off the path of your dreams and destiny. I've already helped many others, such as family, friends, random strangers, patients, social media followers, and friends as they travel along this life journey to make their dreams a reality. I feel that the time is right to share my story because of the many obstacles I have overcome to achieve my goals and dreams of becoming a doctor and living my life to the fullest while enjoying my passion for travel.

As you read my book, you will see that my approach to life is simple. One day, it dawned on me that kids seem to be the happiest people on earth. Their carefree and genuine ways make us adults seem to have lost the essence of living. I genuinely believe that if we are more childlike—not childish—we will reach our maximum potential for true happiness.

Let us take a look at some of the natural character-istics that business coach Nigel Williams has stated that kids like:

- Having fun—They continually look for ways to enjoy everything they do.
- Constantly asking questions—They want to know "why?"
- Laughing a lot—They find something humorous about the simplest things.
- Being positive—They find good in everything.
- Being physically active—They never stop or are dis-tracted until something better comes along.
- Being creative and innovative—They use their imagination every day.

- Daring to dream—To them, nothing is impossible.
- Learning enthusiastically.
- Being adaptable and flexible—They are always open to change.
- Expressing emotions—They share with others honestly and daringly.
- Not worrying for long periods—They don't brood on negativity.
- Believing in themselves and their ability to achieve.
- Resting when they are tired—They are in touch with their bodies.
- Taking risks—They aren't afraid to keep trying something they aren't initially good at, e.g., walking as babies.
- Behaving childlike, not childish.
- Being passionate about a lot of things.

https://www.linkedin.com/pulse/
childrens-natural-characteristics-twist-nigel-williams/

As you read my book, my goal is to challenge you to identify and incorporate these behaviors into your life. These behaviors will make you question your belief system, evaluate unhealthy thoughts, release the hidden power within you to accomplish your dreams and desires, and guide you into creating better habits that will lead to a happier, healthier, and more fulfilling lifestyle.

As a physician, I have come in contact with individuals from all walks of life, from the super-wealthy to the homeless/unhoused. Each one has taught me lessons I have taken with me along my journey and helped shape who I am. I have learned that when you take time to connect with others, you will gain much more than you can imagine. Maintaining a positive attitude with individuals leaves an imprint on your heart that will resonate with your soul and improve your life. Your positive behavior is limitless; it will inspire each person you come in contact with, who will pass that inspiration on to someone else. So, the more positive imprints there are, the more your chance of returning positivity to your life.

Life is filled with many uncertainties and struggles. We are not guaranteed a perfect life. Traveling along my journey has been trying, and because of it, I am much more grateful for all I have today. Whether it's childhood trauma, divorce, breakups, layoffs, or illness, there are many factors in life that we have no control over. I want to share my struggles because my lessons have led to my blessings. I aim to share my ups and downs and everything in between to help you realize you can live the life you deserve. I want to share my story so no matter where you are in your life, you will know it is never too late to start your journey. If you are not equipped to handle the adversities in life, you can become overwhelmed and despondent.

As a physician, speaker, coach, and entrepreneur, I am on a mission to inspire and empower you to live your divine purpose and to choose happiness and joy. I want you to understand that God is truly in control, and you must trust that He wants you to live your best life. He will give you the power to create a fulfilling life. I have gained wisdom and want to help give you the strength to win. My book will show that naysayers will not stop you from achieving your dreams. Your struggles will not define you; you can grow and succeed because you are not a quitter. I want to spark the fire in you that will propel you to overcome any obstacles or challenges life throws you. My book will be like your best friend, empathize with your pain, tears, failures, and disappointments, and remind you that you are an OVERCOMER. In an evocative meander through my life struggles, I share my gift of perspective as a lifelong overcomer and provide you with *The Prescription for Overcoming*. When you read this book, you will walk away with:

- Finding your authentic self.
- Tools to discover your divine purpose.
- Knowledge of your self-worth.
- Realizing that quitting is not an option.
- The art of turning your setbacks into comebacks.
- Understanding that a positive mindset is key to maintaining a fulfilling life.

Whosoever trusteth in the Lord, happy is he.
Proverbs 16:20

I will praise thee; for I am fearfully and wonderfully made.
Psalms 139:14

CHAPTER ONE

Know Thyself

"It's a girl!" the nurses shrieked. After three years of trying to conceive, I was born after an emotionally suppressed nine-month pregnancy and a very long and painful childbirth. I was chosen to be the womb opener, the first child born after a struggle with difficulty conceiving or infertility. From an early age, girls and women are surrounded by societal expectations of motherhood. Becoming a mother is not as natural and can be difficult for some. But finally, the suffering and emotional turmoil were over, and a name was selected. The meaning of Annetta, God has favored me, was a perfect choice from the baby name book. After all, my mother achieved her highest aspiration and found great joy and happiness in being a mom. For her, her true essence was defined by the art of raising a child, with the best parts being giving baths, combing hair, going on strolls, dressing, feeding, and carrying her child.

As I began to grow, similarities between each parent became more evident. With an easygoing and calm temperament, I typically only hollered for food and sleep as expected. Childhood is when you learn who you are, your feelings, how to walk and talk, and how to understand the world around you. I enjoyed being playful and adventurous, and hiding between supermarket aisles became one of my favorite pastimes.

As a firstborn, I automatically fell into my role to please and achieve. Being well-behaved was second nature, and the grades came without effort. As I became more aware of myself and who I was, I saw myself as a daughter of immigrants who had to learn to act and speak differently from my parents to avoid being teased. I was able to expand my imagination as my dad frequently challenged me with questions about faraway lands. He engrained in me the desire to see more: cultures, peoples, and places. Even though travel costs proved too great a financial strain for my parents, I had world puzzle maps and imagination for free.

Aunty Alice, a constant presence in our upbringing, had given us this gift—a reversible world and the United States of America puzzle map. This tangible gift helped develop my love of traveling and to experience cultures of distant lands. At the very young age of five, I had the privilege of traveling to the island of St. Lucia to visit the maternal side of my family. I do not remember much from this trip, but I know it left a lasting impression on who I am today. Various aspects of my life, including this family trip I took at a young age, have inspired my love for traveling.

My dad instilled in me that my environment should never define me. It was an environment where, unfortunately, teasing was inevitable. However, surprisingly, it changed my life for the better because it molded my character in a way that I could be proud of. I was surrounded by many aunties and uncles who were present for every graduation and achievement. This support only positively impacted my childhood and helped to shape my resilience and optimistic nature toward life experiences.

Your trauma, past pain, or struggles do not define you. You should not define yourself or let anyone define who you are. You are not defined by where you are from or where you grew up. You are not the person who grew up in that bad neighborhood. I grew up in what felt like a dangerous neighborhood known for its high crime rate. These experiences are part of my story that made me who I am, but they do not define me. These experiences that you may have experienced while growing up in a particular town, city, or neighborhood have made you stronger, wiser, and more resilient, but it is not who you are.

Growing up, I never felt that my neighborhood defined me because my parents had instilled in us the confidence we needed. We walked the streets daily after school with our heads raised proudly of who we were and our heritage - children of Saint Lucian immigrants. There will always be people in your life who will judge and criticize you and say things based on the bits and pieces of information that they know about you. However, it does not reflect who you genuinely are. Those people try to insult and criticize you based on who they *think* you are. They are only reflections of their current toxic mental state and level of self-awareness. It is only their perception and opinion; you should never define yourself based on what others think of you. Don't let the way they see you change who you are. The next time someone makes you feel you are not good enough, underestimates your abilities, or looks down on you, remember King David and his boldness in approaching Goliath. David did not look at his abilities but depended solely on his faith in God to deliver him from Goliath. In the same way, you should not depend on your own strengths and abilities but surrender to God to overcome your daily battles and struggles of life. God is good and great and will lift and carry any burden placed before you.

Believe in yourself and do what is best for you. Be firm and steadfast in your decisions and your belief in God. Be happy and grateful for being who you are and your impact on others. Be your authentic self. Instead, aspire to be powerful, loving, and undefinable. Undefinable means that you cannot be defined or predictable by anyone else but God. Our behaviors are powered by emotions such as fear and ambitions. The more others can predict your daily patterns and habits, the more likely they will be able to figure out your weaknesses. For example, after a few observations of your behavior, you can become an easy target for a home burglary. Being predictable will allow you to be exploited for your expected behavior. Limit the ability for others to expose your weaknesses by allowing God to work on you constantly. At any point in your life, you are a work in progress, unpredictable, continually changing, and undefinable.

As a young adult lady, I grew up with the unconditional support of both my parents and a strong center in family orientation. I was blessed with the luxuries of safety, security, and love, and I am forever thankful. Although I am responsible for the decisions and actions of my life, my family has played a significant role in how I carry myself and the aspirations I set for myself. Having a supportive family made my life easier to endure during rough patches and made it easier for me to reach my goals.

I've endured heartaches and painful memories, but I am never alone in my pain. I think my family is the direct cause of my naturally elevated confidence during vulnerable phases in my life. This support created a mindset that helped me overcome the most challenging patches and come out on top. Although all families are unique in their set of dynamics and dysfunction, they all impact a child's mental, physical, and emotional development.

As humans, we are multidimensional and have so many sides. Sometimes, one person may know one side and another person the other. As a physician, I must say I have a professional side. Then there's the crazy, funny, outgoing side that my family sees. Yet when we peel back all those layers, who are you really? Who is your core being? Have you ever asked yourself that question? How do others see you? How do they describe you? Are you willing to let others see who you actually are? Once you have discovered your true being, the path and direction of your life will become apparent. You can make decisions for your life and know what's best for you. You become in tune with your desires and can recognize them when they are present in various forms. You will also gain confidence in being open and sharing your authentic self with others. Others will appreciate your presence and what you genuinely bring to the table.

Despite all the adventurous and living-on-the-edge situations, I always knew in the back of my mind I needed to succeed. Growing up, I had this inner drive to be anything I wanted and was always motivated by my home, church, and school circles.

As we go through life's journey, there are no guarantees in the outcomes except the results of what we put in. These results, whether positive or negative, are part of the uncertainty of life. However, once we become in tune with our inner desires and goals, life flows in the direction that brings us the most happiness and fulfillment. We should never be afraid to take time alone and away from the everyday stresses to learn and understand our soul's desires. We all know what is best for us deep down within, though we often ignore our intuitions. As you develop a healthy relationship with yourself and get to know yourself, you will also learn and discover your inner child—the part of yourself that is carefree and without fear. With frequent coaching and self-dialogue, you will begin to enjoy who you really are as a person. This process can be enlightening, scary, and fun all at the same time. The goal is to have fun in the process and journey, and you will be free to choose happiness.

On the other hand, you may be at a point in your life where you may not realize that you do not know who you truly are, or you may feel that things are going pretty okay and there is no need for change unless it's brought to your attention as was done to me. At what I now retrospectively see as the fork in the road of my life, I was posed with the question that set the path for my life.

You may encounter mental blocks as you focus on who you are and what you want for yourself. This is where close family, friends, and significant others may play a role in getting you on the right path of your journey. As I became excited about a new goal, I always reached out to my mother. I have always trusted her wisdom and advice. So don't be afraid to ask others who know you relatively well and can give you honest feedback. You will be amazed at what others think and know about you and your desires.

Your relationship with God and yourself sets the tone for every other relationship. God created you in His image—a masterpiece. God knew you before you were born and had a plan for yourself for you to succeed. It does not matter where you were born, how you were born, or the circumstances of your birth; you were born for a reason and a purpose. Now, your goal is to figure out that purpose. Once you do, you will live a life filled with inner joy, peace, and happiness. One way to identify your purpose is to connect with God, your creator. If He created the masterpiece, he must know *why* he created it. Many individuals understand their purpose and run as far away from it as possible, realizing they continue to search for happiness in the wrong things. Many others are just going through the motions, not realizing that they are not living up to their full potential or not living out their purpose. Remember, you are talented, beautiful, blessed, capable, and equipped.

But as for you, be strong and do not give up, for your work will be rewarded.
2 Chronicles 15:7

CHAPTER TWO

Know Your Worth

id my parents have any idea what their first daughter would be like? A daughter who was hungry to learn, with the desire to succeed, rise above failures, take the unbeaten path, have a passion for world travel and cultures, and be an inspiration for others. Did they know or have any suspicion? What was their dream for me? Growing up as a first-generation Virgin Islander, I had Saint Lucian parents who bravely left the comfort of their homeland and families to start a new life in a foreign country. I could imagine my dad leaving the island of St. Lucia and his family and friends behind at age twenty-four, eager to start a better life out of bare necessity and not for fun or leisure. I wonder how he felt boarding a plane for the first time when he traveled to St. Croix, US Virgin Islands. Was he as terrified as I am when flying in small planes? What was it like when he landed?

The culture shock he may have experienced could have caused him to feel homesick, or did he feel like it needed to be done? What was it like for him looking for a job? Was he discriminated against because of where he came from or because of the way he spoke? Before long, my mother joined my father and uprooted her life away from her parents. Being the last of twelve children to leave her parents' home, this must have been very traumatic. I could imagine the heartbreak she felt leaving her parents behind to join my dad in an unknown territory. Did she cry or have anxiety as she left for a better life? Was she able to communicate with her parents frequently once she left? How did my grandparents feel once she left, and now they were alone? Or were they content as their other children had left and already created their paths in different foreign lands?

My mother was not starting totally in the dark as my dad had already had several years under his belt and had likely already had a handle on his new way of life. He had already had multiple jobs and dared to refuse work on sugarcane plantations cutting sugar cane at one job. He was determined to work in the boiler room, which was a higher risk, and received more pay. He skillfully got his work permit through another employer, whom he advised that it was illegal for him to hire workers for an extended period without providing his staff with proper work documentation. With his work permit in hand, he worked his way to the oil refinery, where he became one of the best heavy equipment operators on the island. What was his drive? What pushed him to want and do better for himself?

Within several years of marriage, my parents started their family and settled into life on St. Croix. Any dreams of making large sums of money and returning to their homeland, St. Lucia were abandoned as my sisters and I started school. Education is the most important aspect in immigrant families, as parents want their children to do and be better than they were. They saw education as the guaranteed way to have a successful life. In their migration journey, they struggled in many instances as the educational system they came from was considered inferior. Fortunately, I did not struggle at school. Learning was second nature, and I loved learning new things and concepts. I spent my summer doing extracurricular educational activities and playing "teacher" to my younger siblings.

At age seventeen, I left my entire life in St. Croix to start college in a small town in Massachusetts. I uprooted my homogeneous culture and left my parents, friends, church family, two younger siblings, and everything that made me who I was up to that point. I wanted to further my education. I wanted a better life. I was excited to leave my small island home and had none other than my dad to plan and accompany me on my journey to college— a privilege that I do not take for granted. If there were one place where a small island girl would experience culture shock, it would be South Lancaster, Massachusetts. Did I have what it took to survive as I journeyed into a new land, the mainland, as it was referred to by us Virgin Islanders? Will my parents' path help me overcome any obstacles that I encounter? Would I have the gumption of my father to maneuver skillfully along my path and achieve my goals?

College, for me, was a significant, life-altering experience. Without a thought, I forgot my inner desire to become a doctor. It just faded away like it never existed. While in high school, I excelled academically and was consistently ahead of the class. However, once I got to college, everything changed. Leaving my homogenous society after high school and entering a mostly Caucasian world, I was slapped immediately with second-class citizen status—a brutal culture shock. Somewhere along the lines, my drive became less noticeable, and I started doing just enough to get by. My environment was slowly changing my attitude and drive, and I was okay with it. Subtly, I was led to believe that I wasn't good enough in more ways than one. Only certain groups of students seem to be passing the chemistry classes. At the time, I thought little of it and slowly became satisfied with making C's to pass.

I soon found out that I was quite the average Jane on campus. That did not sit right with me, nor was it the person I had set out to be. I was able to cope with my new environment, culture, and climate. It opened a whole new world of people and experiences that I thoroughly enjoyed despite prejudice and discrimination. Attending college in a predominantly white school was not for the faint of heart, especially for a girl like me, or was it? Like my parents, I got through it as if it were my only option. Somehow, I did not fully understand racism and its impact on my psyche. I had never heard the word before arriving to the mainland or had never been on it's receiving end. It was there as I sensed it but somehow buried in the depth of my emotional experience.

Growing up in the Virgin Islands, where being black is not a minority, I never felt short of role models or thought that I couldn't be whatever I wanted to be. My parents did not have much, but they worked hard to give us the best they could. They couldn't afford to pay for my college tuition, so along with getting loans, I juggled several jobs. I woke up at 4 a.m. before the break of dawn to join the team at my college janitorial department. I stocked shelves at the local grocery store. Eventually, I landed a less demanding job at my school's library. I continued marching to the beat of my own drum and eventually settled into the idea of being an average Jane. It was not until many years later that I fully understood how racism and discrimination affected who I was, my dreams, and my goals. I later transferred to a different college in another state, allowing me to experience another subculture. This is when the effects of my first college experience would manifest itself.

Out of nowhere, feelings of self-doubt and feeling "less than" began to creep in. I started doubting my initial dreams of becoming a doctor. That inner feeling of not being good enough had replaced my instinct to know instinctually that I could do anything I chose to without a doubt. I had no idea where this feeling came from, and

I never actually acknowledged that it was present. Yet that feeling caused me to say no to becoming a doctor with all the excuses I could find: medical school is too long, I need to make money now, or I just didn't want to do it anymore. There was no logical explanation for giving up on my dream, but I did.

In many ways, my life experiences were similar to those of my parents. One is that we both left our homes for better opportunities. It was also very different because they had already done it and left a footprint for me to follow. I am genuinely grateful for their path and the leap of faith they took to spread their wings so I could soar and become who I am and truly know my worth. I now know my worth and act accordingly, never settling for less than I deserve.

Once you have given up on your dream, you will become uneasy as you run from your purpose. On that road to seeking a future along with happiness, I was searching for my calling. I always knew I wanted to go to college and get a career to one day become successful in the medical field. I searched for my passion in life—a passion for helping others since I was little. I felt that perhaps my calling had to do with people. I believe everyone has a talent that can help their community and ultimately affect the world. Sometimes, what we strongly believe in is worth fighting for, and we will do the impossible to achieve it. Besides fulfilling my intended profession, I wanted to fulfill my purpose as a Christian. Imagine a life without limitations on what you can be, have, or do. Your value is priceless, and your potential is limitless.

Without much ado, I completed my college degree. I moved back home, another indication of being privileged, unlike my parents, who, up to this point, had abandoned any thoughts of returning to their homeland. Being at home gave me a sense of belonging that I needed and had been deprived of for the past five years of my life. I quickly got a job in my field as a Laboratory Scientist at the local hospital. Before long, my time at home began to ignite my true sense of value and worth. This was the beginning of what would place me on the path to live the life God created me to have fully. This spark made me realize I was not fulfilling my potential.

If others do not see your worth, it doesn't make you unworthy. Set your affirmation that you are ENOUGH and believe it with every ounce of your being and in your heart. It is the only path to securing the peace, joy, and freedom you deserve. You are worth every good thing and blessing that comes your way because God created you and placed you in this world for a purpose. Embrace your worth, and never doubt your place in this world. Let your light shine along your life's journey so that others may see your purpose and glorify God.

I can do all things through Christ
who strengthens me.
Philippians 4:13

CHAPTER THREE

Eat "NO" for Breakfast

"You will NEVER get into medical school!" she said as I gasped internally at the harshness and pain of the words as they pierced my inner core. *"How could she be so mean?"* I thought. To make matters worse, she said it in front of everyone. The shame and embarrassment I felt was indescribable. My supervisor was stern and rigid, especially with this part-time student working in the laboratory. As an undergraduate student studying Medical Technology/Clinical Laboratory Science, my advisor thought that to help me pass the board exam, I should get practical experience. He found a job approximately twenty minutes from my college. Although it was every other weekend, I worked until 11 p.m., and public transportation was unavailable afterward. I did not let this minute factor cause me any despair because where there is a will, there is a way. I trusted my advisor and appreciated that he went out of his way to help me. I surely did not want to disappoint him, and most importantly, I also wanted to pass my boards. So, every other weekend, I would miss usual college activities such as basketball games, but my friends would come and pick me up many times, up to five at a time, or they would show up in multiple vehicles. Little did I know that this job that I was so grateful for would change the trajectory of my life path and future.

One day, while discussing my plans with my supervisor, I expressed my desire to attend medical school. She was intrigued and immediately interjected with the inquiry into my grade for organic chemistry. I proudly said, "a C," as I had worked tirelessly to pass and had to repeat the class previously. She blurted out, "You will never get into medical school!" At that very moment, I was traumatized. I do not recall the remainder of the conversation or what happened afterward.

I eventually graduated in August of 1995 with my Bachelor's degree in Medical Technology, passed my board exam, and returned home to work with no plans of furthering my education or following my dream to become a doctor. Working in the lab was routine and monotonous, but I was grateful for my first real job. As fate would have it, the desire to do more slowly began creeping into my mind. I questioned myself about what I needed to do. It wasn't medicine because it was already etched in my mind that I could never be a doctor.

With intense and agonizing soul searching, I decided that pursuing a Master of Public Health was the answer because becoming a doctor was a nonissue. I thought to myself, *"That will be great. At least it is close to medi-cine."* I applied to numerous schools, only to be rejected by each one. How was I to get ahead if they won't accept me? *"Additionally, this is my dream and purpose,"* I thought. Eventually, Virginia Commonwealth University in Richmond, Virginia, initially gave me provisional acceptance. I was ecstatic about this opportunity to further my education, which I started in August 1997.

Once I arrived in Richmond, I realized living in the United States as a graduate student was more complicated than I thought. I was unprepared for what I was about to face. I could not get any housing because I was unemployed, and the university provided no housing for graduate students. I eventually stayed in a hotel nearby but had to leave as I had exhausted the $10,000 I had saved while working for almost two years back home. I informed the university that I was basically homeless and desperately begged them to allow me to stay in the dormitory with the undergraduate students. As belittling as it felt, I had no other options and was humble and grateful for a place to stay. I rarely discussed that I was a graduate student and seldom made friends with anyone in the dormitory.

When walking from class with my peers, I would walk past the dormitory so no one would know where I lived because the sheer embarrassment of not being able to have my own apartment was too much. Once classes were over in May, they informed me that the dormitory would be closed. With a few months left before I completed my degree, I began looking for an apartment to sublet. This meant finding the perfect apartment. Perfect in that the individual would leave at the end of the semester but had exactly three months left on their lease—nothing more, nothing less. After intense searching, God made it possible for me to find that exact apartment—one with three months left on the lease. *"Perfect!"* I thought. My sister could join me, as she had completed her degree back home in the Virgin Islands and decided she wanted to explore life on the mainland.

I was so focused on my drive, knowing that this was what I would need to feel completely fulfilled and whole, that I completed my Master of Public Health in August 1998, exactly one year later. As much as I struggled to get this degree, I did not even care to attend my graduation once I finished. I felt nothing.

At the time, I did not realize what I was experiencing was a part of normal human psychology. I felt like this because I was looking for happiness in something that couldn't provide happiness. My desires and efforts were misdirected because I did not know what happiness was or how to obtain it. At this point, I realized I was ready to find true happiness; until now, nothing in life could fulfill what I sought. To understand why life feels unsatisfactory or meaningless, you need to understand happiness and the meaning of life. True happiness is unconditional and doesn't disappear because your circumstances may change. Being aware of this can help you find ways to be

grateful and experience ongoing satisfaction and fulfillment from the things you have.

If I thought going to graduate school was difficult, my
next experience would top it. Naturally, one looks for a
job in your field after completing a degree. So why was I
not able to obtain a job? I'd hear the same thing: *interview after interview, rejection after reflection, we will call
you after we will call you*. When would I get a break?
It certainly wasn't soon. As my sublet lease began to
expire, I needed a place to stay, and without a job, I was
back at square one. My sister and I prayed for things to
get better. I thought this would definitely work because
at least two of us were praying versus me praying alone.

The day we packed up the U-Haul, we had nowhere
to go. While aimlessly driving, my sister suddenly
remembered she knew someone who lived about one
hour away and had an empty home. She called him, and
he informed us we could stay there, but he would need
to come later to address any repairs in the house that
may be necessary. We did not care, as we would at least
have a roof over our heads. The best part was he told us
we did not have to pay rent until we found jobs. Wow!
God took care of this. Still, no jobs were lining up, and
money was scarce. I was embarrassed to call home to
ask for help because my mom's first response would be
to return home. We struggled instead to the point of
not eating for three whole days. After the first twenty-
four hours, the hunger pangs began to wear off. By day

three, we reached out to a local Seventh-day Adventist Church, and a lovely Sister from the church came by with three bags of groceries that we made to last for weeks. Although we did not eat canned foods growing up, my sister and I appreciated the canned foods from the church's pantry.

Finally, the landlord arrived, and we were able to share our dilemma of job hunting, lack of finances, and lack of food. He empathized with us and suggested that moving to a bigger city might help. His solution was that I should move to Kansas City, where it would be easier to find a job. I again agreed to take that leap of faith to explore uncharted territory. Our conversations kept us awake on that thirteen-hour drive from Virginia to Kansas City. The hissing sound of driving on the highway was silenced as we delved into deeper conversation. I was posed with the question, "If there was one thing you wanted to be, what would it be?"

Without hesitation, I answered, "A doctor!" I had no idea where that response came from. I had stifled that desire and never thought about it until now. Up to that point, I never imagined it was possible. I never prepared for it. The thought had been obscured in the back of my mind after my supervisor's remark dazed me when informing me I would never be a doctor. My friend then posed the follow-up question: "So why aren't you?" Shocked by the question, I did not have a response. His repeated question, "Yes, so why aren't you a doctor?" really sunk into my inner core. Deep down inside, it's who I wanted to be, but I wasn't. Why was I not following my dream? Why was I ignoring my heart's desire? Why didn't I feel the passion? Or was I avoiding my greatest fear and substituting that desire with other things?

Sure enough, within two weeks, as my friend had promised, I secured a job as a Clinical Laboratory Scientist. Obviously, working in public health was not in God's plan. God, being a perfect God, had a different plan to fulfill His will in my life. Shortly after, I purchased a Jaguar XJ6 with personalized license plates because, after all those trials, I deserved it. The horizon looked great, and I could finally get my very own apartment. I immediately informed my sister, whom I had left behind in Virginia, to come to Kansas City, where she also could secure employment and eventually her own vehicle—finally, a string of yeses!

We often try to force things and don't wait for God's timing. It's a constant struggle. It's a burden. You can't seem ever to take off. However, when you let go and let God do it his way, in his timing, there is an ease and effortless nature in its completion. God will give you the strength you need, and you will feel peace as his favor directs you into his plan.

My confidence grew as I began settling into my new life with my new vehicle and my new job in the lab. I made new friends and started learning a new language because of the influx of Spanish immigrants migrating from Texas. Keeping the conversation from the drive to Kansas City in the back of my mind, I knew it would be now if there was a time to tackle becoming a doctor seriously. I began looking into the steps and realized I was considered a nontraditional student because I did not go directly from undergraduate to medical school. *"That was fine,"* I thought.

I also realized that I needed additional pre-med classes. I registered at the University of Kansas City and secured a pre-med advisor. I felt that my pre-med advisor was neither for me nor against me. She did her job as she guided me through the steps. With much more confidence, I aced my pre-med classes and began applying to medical school. As a nontraditional student with a full-time job paying well and minimal expenses, I had the funds to apply to medical school. So, to increase my chances of acceptance, I applied to many schools only to receive rejection letters from every school. I told myself that's expected as a nontraditional student, and from what many were saying, including my advisor, it takes a few tries.

The following year, I decided to take a leave from my job and register for a summer medical program at Howard University to strengthen my application. What an excellent opportunity to be surrounded by like-minded individuals on a medical campus. We were all nontraditional students from all walks of life. For the first time, I did not feel that I was alone on this journey. There were so many out there going through the same thing. There was no turning back, and I was sure that adding this to my resume was a no-brainer for acceptance. If anything, program directors would see my determination, zeal, and resilience. The deal was sealed, and I had to become a doctor. I had done way too much to turn back now. Again, I applied the second time, adding not only allopathic schools but also osteopathic schools, only to get more no's and rejection letters from every single school. Between the two application cycles, I applied to hundreds of schools. I was utterly devastated to read the words: *Dear Applicant, We are sorry to inform you ...* There was no need to continue reading after that point.

Why did God place this burning desire in me and make me go down this path, only to allow me to experience rejection after rejection? Why? Yet something in me was not allowing me to give up. I kept going as if I was a glutton for punishment.

One day, my friend came to me and said there was another way to get into medical school. My ears perked up to hear that it would require me to leave the United States and study in the Caribbean in Spanish. Really? My mind flooded with so many questions. Is this what I would have to do? Is anyone else doing this? Why me? I certainly wasn't making any headway with learning Spanish. The idea sounded so foreign that I said it would take a year to consider.

After one year, I was convinced that this was the path I needed to follow. I decided to make the move to the Dominican Republic. This was my "now or never." I had chartered into unknown territory before, and it felt natural and easier by this time. Again, I was embarrassed about this decision but knew it had to be done, like almost being homeless in Virginia and having to live in the undergraduate dormitory. I told no one except family members and a few close friends, who I instructed to keep my move a secret.

I completed the four-page medical school application booklet provided to me in English. I immediately thought this might not be so bad if there was an English application. The application process was seamless and seemed too good to be true.

A few individuals who knew I was going to make the leap felt I was crazy to move to a foreign country where I did not speak the language or know anyone. Regardless, I decided that this was where I would attend medical school. Who did I think I was? Did that audacity come from my dad? Was this God's perfect timing to fulfill his purpose in my life? You must realize that you must make the right decision even though others may think your decision to follow your dream is crazy. I want you to know that you do not have to subscribe to the myths about how you should live, what you should have, and by what age you should have it, especially for women. I permitted myself not to fit into society's mold and connected with what I needed to survive and thrive.

Be strong and courageous. Do not be frightened, and do not be dismayed, for the Lord your God is with you wherever you go.
Joshua 1:9

CHAPTER FOUR

You Are Not a Quitter

Once I arrived in the Dominican Republic, I realized the magnitude of what was facing me. As the taxi picked me up from the airport and got onto the highway, I immediately knew that deciding to study medicine in a foreign country would be extremely challenging. I began questioning my decision as we traveled approximately thirty miles along the bumpy, white caliche path. I wondered if I made the biggest mistake of my life. *"What if this did not work out?"* I thought. My taxi driver and I did not speak to each other because my attempts to learn Spanish were futile, and I could not converse past the word "Hola." His frequent stares through the rearview mirror made me wonder if he also wondered if I knew what I was getting into.

He took me to a hotel, and I was left in bewilderment by being unable to communicate and feeling alone and isolated. Feeling immensely terrified and crippled with fear, I came up with a plan to proceed. I attended church on the weekend, one I was familiar with, because I felt it would be the safest option. I chose the same denomination I grew up in and the one that came through for my sister and me after we went three days without food in Virginia. As a foreigner, luckily, I stood out like a sore thumb. As if God was orchestrating this scene, I unknowingly sat beside the only English-speaking church member. We began chatting, and I explained to her my situation of just arriving in the country, not being able to speak the language, and not having a place to stay. She said, "Do not worry. I will help you". Such relief filled my soul when I realized that God sent an angel. She kept her word, and within days, she was able to assist me in securing an apartment. This process included getting a lawyer to draft the rental contract and connecting the lights.

Things were slowly progressing, and I was elated to get the keys to my very own apartment. I still did not feel entirely comfortable with the whole situation. I was grateful for the roof over my head, but turning on the electricity was a process. I couldn't call the electrical company and let them know I lived alone without family or friends in a foreign country because they probably couldn't care less. Each day, I patiently waited. I dreaded nightfall as there were no lights to turn on. The surrounding neighbors knew there was a new tenant, and she was a foreigner who did not speak the language. While in the apartment, I could only eat food that didn't need refrigeration. Also, I was too scared to venture out to purchase food. Eventually, after two weeks, my situation became too much to bear.

I made a quick phone call home in despair and tears, expressing to my mother that I couldn't go through with this and I couldn't handle it anymore. My mother listened and said, "It's okay. You can come home if you want until they install your electricity." In addition, I had a few more weeks before school started. I took her up on the offer and headed to the comfort and solace of home, where planting my feet has always invigorated and grounded me with strength and purpose. Before becoming too comfortable at home, I received a call from my new church member friend in the Dominican Republic that they had installed my lights. I was overjoyed and made preparations to head back. I had enough fuel in my tank to tackle a few more adversities that may come my way.

Before long, medical school quickly started, and I became familiar with other foreigners on a similar path as mine. I began to feel less alone on this journey. As everyone bustled to their classes, each had their own story of arriving in the Dominican Republic to study medicine. The diversity was enchanting, and I appreciated the opportunity to learn about their stories. Students came from India, Persia, Barbados, Puerto Rico, Haiti, the United States, Canada, Cuba, and various countries of Africa, such as Nigeria, Cameroon, and Ghana, to name a few. We were all with one mission and desire—to become doctors.

I quickly learned that everyone was not starting on the same playing field. The medical school in the Dominican Republic was structured as a BS/MD program in the United States. Students could start medical school right after high school, some even as young as fifteen. Coming in with a bachelor's and master's degree from the US, I received credit for many classes. Any confidence that gave to me was stripped away during class when I could not understand anything the professor recited and when students openly laughed at me because I did not speak the language. Individuals who attend medical school are typically competitive, and getting help from other students is as difficult as finding a needle in a haystack. The lucky ones, mainly the foreign male students, could obtain photocopied notes after class, which they secretly shared with me.

Since many of my classes varied with other foreign students, I could not always depend on that strategy. I decided that I would have to start taking my own notes. At first, they did not make sense as I listened intently and wrote what I heard with surety. There were a few snickering and side-eyes from other students because they knew my language barrier, but I kept at it as if my life depended on it. Like magic, before the semester was over, I had perfected my note-taking. It became second nature, and my note-taking skills were top-tier. Once I mastered note-taking in Spanish, Spanish-speaking students began asking me to copy my notes. This gave me that temporary boost I needed as an international student on this rite of passage to become a doctor in a foreign land.

Each following semester was a struggle. There seemed to be a hefty price to pay as an international student. As I grew to understand, many professors, students, and even administrative staff felt that foreigners were at an advantage, so there were willful attempts to make our lives difficult. Most likely, not every foreign student experienced this, but I certainly did. Simple situations turned into unattainable tasks, such as difficulty registering for a particular class that I needed to proceed to the next semester, missing exam dates or assignments due to miscommunication, erroneous grades being reported, and changing curriculums, to name a few. This led to frequent trips to the administrative office, pleading for a resolution to each problem. It was constant, and the burden sometimes became heavy and difficult. My only hope was to pray and cry to God to allow each situation to pass and for the strength to go through it.

Many days, I cried because I felt I couldn't go any further. On one of those days, I called my mother, who has always been my strength and number one supporter. It was a Saturday, and she was at church. She walked out of the church to take my call because if her daughter calls when she's in church, it must be an emergency. I could hardly express myself to her through the tears, but the gist she got was that I couldn't take it anymore, and I was willing to give up. Why do I need to go through all this?

What was the purpose? It all seemed unfair. I wanted to go home again.

My mother listened intently to her daughter's woes and softly and gently stated, "It's okay. You can come home, but remember, you are not a quitter." Somehow, those words resonated through my core. I made a promise to myself to never complain about my difficult journey. It was mine, and I had to give it my all. As the womb opener, I understood the honor and privilege of being her child, and I was grateful to have received her love, guidance, consoling, and prayers throughout my life. It was my job to make her proud.

The more difficult it is to reach your destination, the more you'll appreciate the journey and the higher your calling will be. Don't give up or give in when you think of quitting or giving up on your calling. That day, my mom also shared a poem with me. She said, "There's a poem in the church bulletin, and I want to read it to you," and this is what she read:

ROAD TO SUCCESS

The road to success is not straight,
There is a curve called Failure,
A loop called Confusion,
Speed bumps called Friends,
Red lights called Enemies,

Caution lights called Family,
You will have flats called Jobs.

If you have a spare called Determination,
An engine called Perseverance,
Insurance called Faith,
A driver called God,
You will make it to a place called Success!

by
Sulaymon Tadese Faozahny

*What things soever ye desire,
when ye pray, believe that ye
receive them, and ye shall
have them.*
Mark 11:24

CHAPTER FIVE

Believe in Yourself

*I*t is so easy to read God's Word and judge how others doubted God when He had proven Himself over and over to them. He performed miracles when the ravens fed Elisha, when the widow's oil multiplied, and He fed hundreds with twenty loaves of bread. God had done the same for me numerous times. He had gotten me this far, and I had slowly been learning to let go of my doubt when circumstances did not go my way. I realized that when things did not work out, God had a better plan, and I would get excited.

After four years of what seemed like constant trials and frustrations, I finally completed medical school. What an accomplishment! At this point, I felt that I could conquer the world. I thought it was the hardest thing I had ever done. I told myself that if I could accomplish this, I could achieve anything I set my mind to. My next task was to apply for residency training upon completing medical school. You must complete a series of exams to get accepted into residency training, where you will train in your specialty. In medical schools in the United States, students must take these exams at various stages as they go through medical school. As a foreign medical student in the Dominican Republic, my school did not provide guidelines or criteria for taking a US exam. International students were on their own for exam preparation, scheduling, etc. Most individuals would typically complete their entire medical education before taking the exams. So, I faced the arduous task of studying for these exams simultaneously. This was certainly not your cup of tea if you were accustomed to being spoon-fed in the educational setting. This system required discipline, grit, gumption, perseverance, resilience, determination, fasting, and praying.

With that attitude, I attempted to take the first exam in the series required to enter specialty training in the United States. I applied for the first exam, USMLE Step 1, the semester before my last. With minimal preparation, I entered the Prometric Center and left more baffled than when I entered. I certainly was not surprised when I received my results: FAIL. Failing step 1 was not a major disappointment for me. I knew I was not fully prepared, but I felt it was a necessary step for me to take to embrace the process of getting into residency. I saw it as a practice run, an expensive one, yet essential to build my motivation to continue. By this point in my life, I was not afraid of failure. My reaction was, *"Now I know exactly how to prepare and study for this exam."* As the saying goes, it is not what happens to you but how you react.

We all have to face hardships and failures at some point. You should not let these difficult times define you, but let your reaction to these situations develop your true character. Every hardship presents as an opportunity and with valuable lessons that can shape your life for the better. Once you understand that the only environment you can control is your internal one, you will sense greater control of your life sooner.

I came up with a rigorous study plan, one that I felt did not lead to failure. Ironically, for the first time, my school also devised a plan to help enrolled students prepare for the exam. Unfortunately, I had just graduated and no longer was enrolled in school. However, I did not let this minor detail deter me from my mission. Unbeknownst to the school, I attended every class provided by an enthusiastic professor whose sublime character and dynamic passion for teaching fueled my love for learning. While diligently attending the course, some individuals offered their advice and tried to discourage me from attending the course, claiming it was a waste of time. I didn't give their opinion a thought as I knew that if a teacher goes above and beyond to inspire my learning, how is my time wasted, and more importantly, why do they care so much that my time is wasted?

It's only to say that when individuals see your desire and drive, it may make them uncomfortable, and they, too, see your success sometimes before you can. These individuals will try to deter you and make you lose focus, but I never allowed it to make me miss a beat. After completing the course, I immersed myself into twelve-hour days of studying for months, starting at 8 a.m. until 10 p.m., with one hour for lunch and dinner. Each day, I flipped through the pages of my Kaplan books, reviewing, highlighting, re-highlighting, and underlining anything I thought could appear on the exam. Tackling questions would help break the monotone of flipping pages. Some made me feel like I would ace the test; other days, I thought I would flunk after completing a set of questions. What are your thoughts?

I only stopped to eat, sleep, and take breaks for my mind to wander. My focus was unwavering, and I visualized myself confidently walking through the halls of a hospital dressed in my white coat. It felt real as I walked under the harsh fluorescent hallway lighting between the bland, neutral walls, absorbing the undertones of artificial soaps and cleansers. My joy and satisfaction mattered most as I saw myself in a purposeful stride. I had never been to the hospital that I envisioned, but it gave me a sense of comfort and peace. I knew this was where I needed to be and promised God that if I could ever walk down that hospital hall, I would never complain about my experience while in residency.

Once I snapped out of daydreaming and returned to reality with my books lying in my lap, my driving force was determination and persistence. My determination and persistence were a product of my belief in myself.

I still believed in the quote written across the wall in my seventh-grade class: Whatever your mind can conceive and believe, it can achieve. I accept this wholeheartedly, and if I fail, I must try again. What better pleasure than to succeed after failing? As echoed by the famous basketball player Michael Jordan, "I've failed over and over again in my life, and that is why I succeed." You can overcome any obstacle or difficulty by staying focused on your goals and desires. I also believe that I was placed on this earth for a purpose—to impact the lives of others.

As Benjamin E. Mays stated, "Every man and woman is born into the world to do something unique and something distinctive, and if he or she does not do it, it will never be done." This quote became even more real to me when I understood that after trying to conceive for three years, my mother received me as a gift from God. No matter the circumstances of your coming into this world, you were meant to be here. Whatever your purpose is in life, you can use it as a ministry to glorify God. You were meant for greatness. Never let anyone extinguish the fire that fuels your passion and purpose. You are stronger, smarter, and more resilient than you think. You can achieve what you believe. It will take determination, persistence, and doing it afraid.

As I continued to persevere, my exam was approaching, and the prayers were being lifted up. I knew I had put in the work and effort and completed my goal of 10,000 practice questions. I gave my first exam all I had, and all I could do at that point was wait for my results.

Without a proper mail system in the Dominican Republic, my scores were sent to my mother's address in the Virgin Islands. It was a major step in my journey so when my mother came to the Dominican Republic to support me after completing my exam I thought nothing of it. She had been my rock to lean on and was always ready to advise, guide and lead me through many of my life problems. So when she handed me my scores and casually informed me over dinner that I had passed, I was overwhelmed with great joy and felt genuine accomplishment. I was even more elated that she was present to share this moment with me. Success without struggles may not feel as sweet. This success was mine and could not be taken away from me. I did the work, and I received the reward. We celebrated and enjoyed the moment. This was precisely what I needed to boost my confidence and motivation to move to the next step.

After a two-week break for mental rest, I needed to move on to the next step and prepare for my second exam, USMLE Step 2—back to my trusty Kaplan books and neon-colored highlighters. Passing the first exam laid the foundation for the second exam. As I began to push through the materials, I didn't feel as much steam as I felt studying for the first exam, but I persisted. This time around, things certainly felt different. I began having difficulty sleeping at night, and I would suddenly wake up with my heart racing. Then, going back to sleep required so much effort. I began playing hymns to fall asleep. I tried placing the Bible close to my head in an attempt to calm my mind to no avail.

After several sleepless nights and lackluster study days, I experienced a breaking point. I felt my heartbeat in my ears as it thudded in my chest. My hands were shaking, and a tingling sensation covered my body. I couldn't stay in the apartment any longer. I had to escape this intense, all-consuming feeling, but where should I go? Obviously, something was wrong with my heart, and I needed immediate attention. I couldn't take it any longer. I took a motorcycle taxi to the hospital to see one of my former cardiology professors. I burst into his class. Seeing my sense of urgency, fear, and bewilderment in my eyes, he said he would see me immediately after class. I waited patiently at his office, not understanding my overwhelming situation. When he arrived, he performed routine cardiac tests and told me everything was normal. He then handed me a prescription that I should fill.

Feeling so relieved I was not dying, I got home without filling the prescription. I took a deep sigh of relief as I tried to release the weight from my shoulders. I finally looked at the prescription: alprazolam! Wait a minute. I uttered softly to myself, "Did I just have a panic attack?" That tremendous feeling in my chest and the unrelenting rhythm of fear screamed, *"panic attack."* At that split second of realization, I decided that there was only one way for me to handle this. With this being my first situation, I determined it would be my last. Standing in the center of my kitchen in front of my sink, I said a prayer to be a better steward of my body and not allow constant strain and chronic stress to take over my body. I reached for a lighter and placed the flame at the bottom diagonal corner while I held the opposite corner. The flame struggled to stay alive, and it slowly smothered the prescription. I quickly dropped the prescription into the sink as the flame got close to my finger and allowed the water to wash the remaining ash down the drain, along with my worries and fears.

We all carry burdens daily, whether it is past trauma, financial loss, loss of a loved one, or life struggles. The mental strain I placed on myself from excessive studying without creating a healthy balance placed a toll on me. This burden could have easily changed my path if I did not recognize that the unhealthy habit could hinder me from embracing my purpose and dream.

Once I returned to studying, I made a shift in my approach. I incorporated more frequent breaks for mental rest and daily walks around my neighborhood. This significantly changed my routine. How could I neglect such a simple yet significant aspect of my well-being? I was so focused on one part of my life that I ignored many others. Maintaining life balance is essential for your overall health. When you're unbalanced, you are out of alignment with your mind and body. You can easily become distracted and overwhelmed by simple tasks, and your health and well-being will suffer. When your life is in alignment, you can focus on your goals. Every individual must strive to maintain a mental, physical, and spiritual balance. You feel grounded, and with that comes mental clarity, motivation, and complete fulfillment of your priorities and desires. Balanced living means achieving optimal health in all aspects of your life: relationships, work, fitness, health, and emotional happiness.

No one can get in the way of what God has planned for you except you. Despite all your challenges, believe that you can overcome them and become unstoppable when you work on your dreams. You've got this!

Delight yourself in the Lord, and he
will give you the desires
of your heart.
Psalm 37:4

CHAPTER SIX

Stepping Out of Your Comfort Zone

Your comfort zone is a beautiful place where nothing ever grows. One of the biggest reasons many procrastinate or never move forward with their life goals is because they are comfortable with their lives. They are comfortable with their routine and don't want things to change. Stepping out of your comfort zone is going into the unknown, which is often scary. Fear is a common emotion and reaction that can hold you back from reaching your full potential, especially when you step out of your comfort zone. It can be paralyzing, preventing you from pursuing your goals and dreams.

However, it is crucial to understand that overcoming fear is not impossible. Conquering fear is a journey that begins with acknowledging your fear. You will note the feelings and symptoms you are experiencing while visualizing the outcome of taking action despite the fear you feel. This courage and determination will push you beyond your comfort zone to take the necessary steps to reach your goal. Overcoming fear is difficult, but you will be rewarded with fulfillment, igniting your self-confidence and growth. Your comfort zone is likely nice and cozy, surrounded by soft cushion pillows all around you, each one representing your fears, limitations, and negative beliefs. It's time to leave your comfy abode and live the life you always wanted.

Along my life journey, I realized that stepping out of my comfort zone and taking risks not guaranteed to work had taught me more about myself and created experiences I would have never had if I had remained comfortable. Each time I did so, I tore down the comfort of the world the way I knew it. I broke down boundaries. I crushed negative thoughts and, most importantly, resisted the urge to return to the area of familiarity and comfort. Each time you take a risk, you will learn and discover who you truly are deep down inside - your authentic self. The part of you that holds the power to propel you to growth, progress, purpose and living your dreams. Some ways to step out of your comfort zone are to meet new people, visit new places, travel to a new country, learn a new language or sport, or try new foods. I did several of these things simultaneously at various times in my life. My passion for traveling has motivated me to discover new places. With each trip, I am compelled to learn new words, experience new customs and tempt my palate with new foods. I become intrigued with the architecture, excited about the culture and fascinated about the people. Imagine if I went to the same place each time. Everything will be familiar and maybe the staff at local restaurants may even know my name and my usual order on the menu. I would feel comfortable and safe but how would I grow and learn about myself if I am not experiencing anything new. I have learned that the risks of diving into the unknown and traveling through unchartered territory have birthed my creativity and inspiration to the path of living a fulfilling life. When you step out of your comfort zone, each new experience will expand your horizon and perspective on life and motivate you to conquer new goals and promote continued growth.

The Cambridge Dictionary defines "comfort zone" as "a situation in which you feel comfortable and in which your ability and determination are not being tested." Here you feel safe and in control. You are not only familiar with the routine but also with the outcome. So naturally, stepping out of your comfort zone should involve a process where your ability and determination are being tested and ultimately make you uncomfortable. Here you will challenge yourself and learn how to overcome those challenges.

The idea of the "comfort zone" dates back to 1908, when Robert M. Yerkes and John D. Dodson performed a psychological experiment. They concluded that to maximize your performance, you need to go past your comfort zone to a zone called Optimal Anxiety. Tapping into your optimal anxiety or fear zone is simply pushing yourself to the next level and accomplishing things you merely dreamed of or doing things you never thought you could or would even attempt. This is the zone that will take you to the ultimate zone of truly living. In this zone, you will face your challenges head on and learn how to overcome them and acquire new life skills.

Moving to a new place is among the most uncomfortable and mentally challenging activity. More often than not, it results in something positive. It was a Sunday morning. I woke up eager and excited to start the day, knowing I would attend my friend's housewarming party. As the excitement wore off, I felt a sense of nervousness creeping in. That's odd! I suspected some of the foreign students from the university would attend, and it was always an adventure when we got together. I got ready as I attempted to brush off my emotions. Today was the day I was going to have a good time.

"Nice to meet you," I responded after several introductions of new faces. Immediately, my nervousness earlier that day made sense, but one introduction stood out. There was something about him that I couldn't quite put my finger on. He seemed mysterious, and I wanted to know more about him. I accepted his offer to teach me how to dance Konpa, a music genre of Haiti. We stepped onto the dance floor—the dining area—while others looked on as our bodies moved in sync with the rhythm of the pulsating beat. As the melody played, he stepped forward and stretched out his arms. I understood the

signal and twirled, ending back into his arms as our bodies moved in the two-step pattern, suggesting that such
a serendipitous performance could only mean there was
chemistry between us.

Peter took me home after the party, and there was
no denying our connection. The next day, Peter visited
with his pit bull, Roc, perched in the front seat of their
drop-top green Jeep Wrangler as if the dog wanted me
to know my place. What a sight to behold! Within weeks,
we felt like we had known each other our whole lives.
I want to think that meeting Peter in the Dominican
Republic was interwoven into God's big plan for my life.
There was no other way for us to meet. He was perfect
for me. Suddenly, life came with ease. Peter's first order
of business was to find me a new apartment. He immediately advised me that the one my church friend found for
me was not located where most international students
lived and was likely not safe for a foreigner, especially
a female. He made me feel safe, protected, and loved.
Peter and I ultimately became inseparable and got married two years later.

Throughout my journey, I depended on my mother as
a source of strength, and now I have the strength and support of my husband. Having completed dental school one
year prior, Peter supported us while I continued to study
for my exams. By the grace of God, I passed my practical board exam and came one step closer to my dream.

If I had played it safe, I would have missed many
opportunities and the life experience of meeting my soul

mate. The only way to step into your divine purpose and live the life of your dreams is to venture out of your comfort zone. You must face your fears, keep an open mind, test your limitations, face challenges, and learn from your experience.

As I became comfortable outside my comfort zone, I recognized I was meant to do great things. As Neale Donald Walsch states, "Life begins at the end of your comfort zone," and mine was taking off. My confidence blossomed as I began researching various specialties, and with my husband's blessing, I decided to combine pediatrics and internal medicine after exploring how it was possible. Combination programs have proven difficult to get into because of their limited programs, competitiveness, rigorous nature, and incorporating a combined training program in less time. I immediately thought that would be perfect for me—a foreign medical graduate.

While most foreign medical graduates apply broadly to as many programs as possible, I was limited to the twenty-five combined internal medicine and pediatrics programs. I certainly was not limited in my goals and purpose. Friends and family became concerned about my decision to apply to a combined program. My mother encouraged me to contact an acquaintance's wife, a family physician, for her feedback. She put me in touch with another family physician on the mainland, an actual program director. "Oh, you are a foreign medical graduate?" he quipped. "And you would like to become a combined internist and pediatrician? That would not be possible." Not only did he tell me that I would not get into the combined program, but he also informed me that I did not have a chance of getting into any residency program and there was nothing he could do to help me. Honestly, for the first time, a negative narrative did not waver my belief. I kindly thanked him and my family's acquaintance's wife for their time.

To remain unwavering in your belief in yourself, be careful not to let others create self-doubt or compare yourself to others. You are unique, and so is your journey. You have a purpose and your gift is meant to be shared with the world. You certainly do not want to miss out on the opportunity to experience the true meaning of your life. Stepping out of your comfort zone will give you the freedom your heart yearns for. Betting on yourself and taking risks will become second nature, and family and friends will never question your decisions. Once you make that change, you will become more courageous and gradually grow into your authentic self.

I confidently submitted my applications and received invites to three residency programs. I was ecstatic because I knew within my heart that I only needed one interview to get in. I had the favor of God that gave me the advantage over the next person, the next person who had "better" scores, a "better" medical school, or a "better" application. God was leading my life, and during the interview process, I knew they were drawn to me because God had already selected me. Sure enough, when the results were announced on Match Day, I was accepted into my number one choice. God had opened the door to infinite possibilities and opportunities, and there was nothing anyone could do about it.

The phone rang, and the excitement in the chief resident's voice from my new residency program sealed the deal. My husband and a few friends gathered in our apartment, waiting for the news. We all screamed, clapped, and jumped in excitement at the good news. It was unbelievable and surreal. It was confirmation that hard work, dedication, and faith in God paid off. As I began receiving emails from other residents in the program congratulating me and providing advice and support before my arrival, I already felt like part of a family. I knew in my heart that it was God who did it.

I quickly remembered the Family Medicine Director who had previously doubted my abilities to get into a combined internal medicine and pediatrics program. I sent a kind note to Mr. Family Medicine Director, thanking him again for his time and sharing my acceptance to my first choice program. Needless to say, he never responded to my email.

After four years of medical school plus one and a half years to study and take my board exams, I was ready to leave my comfortable, quaint family of friends, my husband, and the new culture I had adopted to attend residency training in the United States.

At this point, my husband and I had been together for five years and married for three years. During this period, we enjoyed being with each other. We did not think or worry about whether we would have a long-distance marriage one day. As with most relationships and marriages, we went through various stages. Sometimes, it went well, while other times, there were bumpy roads. Whatever the situation, we held on to each other because it was always us against everything or everyone else. Sometimes, we felt we had to hold on to each other to survive. We had determined that divorce was never an option.

Four years of residency training was grueling, to say the least, but I never wavered on my promise to God that if I were accepted, I would never complain. The demand from senior staff, colleagues, and the attending was sometimes overwhelming. The sheer volume of work required in residency tested my promise almost daily. Life as a medical resident challenged me both physically and mentally. At the beginning of our separation, my husband and I slept via video call every night for several years. We continue to speak to each other frequently throughout the day. Despite the challenges, I remained excited to learn and practice what I studied and sacrificed so hard for, and I was grateful for the opportunity. As an aspiring internist and pediatrician, I felt blessed to walk the halls I envisioned years prior and be part of a team providing quality care to patients. This opportunity and my graduation from the program in June 2011 represented the culmination of all the hard work and sacrifices made along my journey.

As stated by my program director during my graduation speech, "Many others will now see you and what you have accomplished, and they will never know what it took for you to get where you are today." Those words resonated with me because I knew my journey there was not easy.

Waking up from my comfortable bed in my new rental home in a world-class gated community, I kneeled for my morning prayer. After a blessed silence, I was fully awake and said my prayers. As I got up from my knees, a nervous excitement filled my chest with palpitations and my stomach with butterflies. This was the morning of my first job as a doctor. It was August 2011. I felt prepared, confident, and self-sufficient two months after completing my four years of medical residency training. A good first job will get you started on the path to future success, and you should embrace the opportunity and take advantage of the experience.

As an outpatient physician in rural North Carolina with the nearest specialist at least thirty minutes away, I learned to manage patients in every specialty, from cardiology to rheumatology, with dermatology being my least favorite. In many ways, my first job helped shape me into who I am today, professionally and personally. It taught me the importance of putting God first, believing in myself, never giving up, appreciating family support, and feeling proud when my hard work pays off.

Before long, the vast, wide-open spaces of the North Carolina countryside compounded my isolation and loneliness. I decided I needed to move outside of North Carolina. As my one-year contract as an outpatient physician in North Carolina ended, I was ready to spread my wings and soar above any obstacles. My experience made me bold and fearless, ready to showcase my God-given talents. This led me to research the ideal place to practice and live. I knew exactly what I wanted: a small city with approximately twenty thousand people, a small airport, a mall, a quaint downtown, and a hospital in Florida. Of course, many towns fit the profile, but one small city stood out. I loved the name and location. I called the local hospital because, of course, they needed me on board.

After many years of doubts and fears, I was ready to take a risk, even though I did not know the outcome. Once again, I was prepared to venture and explore another territory. I called the physician recruiter for the hospital. He informed me that no positions were available, but I should call him in six months. Although I did not get the response I wanted, this leap of faith opened the door to the possibility that one day, I could work at the hospital. I noted the date on my calendar to call the physician recruiter and six months from that date, I placed the call as promised. The physician recruiter appeared shocked that I called and did not have any good news for me but decided to interview me regardless, I believe, because of my tenacity and perseverance. I believed in myself and wanted to get my foot in the door and make that first lasting impression. I trusted that this was God's will for me, and I was willing to take the risk because my intuition felt the personal growth, development, and rewards I would experience once I was pushed out of my comfort zone.

To ensure there was no room for error, I researched the hospital's mission, vision, and physicians and knew that I needed to look the part. With the support of my sister and her family, we decided on the minute details and left nothing to chance down to the straightening of my natural hair the night before the interview. Having the uncanny ability to relate to almost anyone, I aced my interview and was offered a position that was never advertised or was available. I was extremely grateful and knew that God was working and placed me in an environment of being the only Black female physician where my talents could be appreciated, developed, and shine.

You can soar like an eagle when you let go of your doubts and fears. Soaring like an eagle means spreading your wings and going after what you believe in with all your heart. The eagle symbolizes strength, renewal, courage, vision, and freedom. You must embrace these attributes to soar higher, farther, and faster toward your goals and dreams.

And I soared. I was recognized in print and on air and served as a trusted and valued medical leader in the community. As I soared higher and higher, I got a glimpse of my full potential. Yet God had other plans once again. Within three years of interacting, socializing, embracing, learning, and giving, I got the urge again. It was that time to leave my comfort zone. I didn't understand the urge. I was doing well. I worked so hard to be where I was. From the Spanish medical classes in the Dominican Republic to the grueling life as a resident training for my specialty, I was ready to give it all up.

It was November 2015, and I was packing up my life and all my belongings to return to the country that gave me this blessed opportunity. This time, I was not nervous, but I was stepping in faith. I was excited about the move as I have always been excited about anything travel-related. I had no idea what my future entailed, and I had no plan. The one sure thing was that I was going back to meet my husband. I was blessed to have a mother who never questioned my decision but only supported my dreams.

My mother learned of my plan to return to the Dominican Republic. She immediately offered to help me move. Many friends and family felt I was packing my hopes and dreams for an unpredictable future. "You are crazy! You will never get this opportunity again! You worked so hard to be where you are. You are going to regret it!" I understood their sentiment because people typically move to another country for a better life and opportunity. Life in the Dominican Republic would not provide me with any obvious opportunity. Yet, I have learned along my life journey thus far that you can learn so much from any drastic lifestyle change as long as you embrace it and make the best of it. As the packing tape ripped off the roll and sealed each box, I packed away fears, doubts, what-ifs, and others' expectations of who and what I was supposed to be.

It built up the anticipation of the unknown, but I was unwilling to live as expected. I was going to create my own path and journey. I was doing it my way. I felt free. I was freed from society's timeline and expectations and honestly did not care what others thought about my decision. People will judge you for everything you do or don't do, so do it anyway. If the price of freedom was being judged, I was ready to pay that price. I kept my eyes on the prize—FREEDOM.

When you step outside of your comfort zone, you are taking a risk of opening yourself to the possibility of stress and anxiety. At this stage in my life, I had stepped out of my comfort zone a few times. Each time, I got nervous when I ventured into uncharted territory, even though I was excited at the same time. Although you may embark on an exciting journey that you have always dreamed of, anxiety tends to creep in, and many times, it will be difficult to distinguish between anxiety and excitement. It has been shown that physiologically, the symptoms of anxiety and excitement are similar: racing heart rate, sweaty palms, tensing up, and the feeling of butterflies in your stomach. We typically associate anxiety with a negative emotion and excitement as a positive emotion.

According to Harvard Professor Alison Woods Brooks, you shouldn't try to calm yourself down when you feel anxious but shift your perspective to a state of excitement. Redirect your focus and get excited about opening your world to new possibilities and challenges. When we are anxious, we feel that everything in our future will go wrong. Excitement is a positive emotion that allows you to welcome the future and its opportunities. I stepped out of my comfort zone with all my emotions and arrived in the Dominican Republic, ready to accept what I had previously known and give up what I had grown accustomed to. But change is a constant in life. Learn to embrace each cycle with joy and excitement. When you feel intimidated about stepping out of your comfort zone, remember that you only feel nervous because it's unfamiliar, not because you are incompetent.

With my mother in the Dominican Republic, my husband and I thought that this would be the perfect opportunity to show her our latest prize possession - a piece of land we had purchased two years prior. We were struggling with the decision whether we should sell it to purchase an apartment or condo because we could not see the vision of building a home pass our limited finances. At this point in our marriage, my husband also saw my mom as a spiritual confidante. We needed her guidance and advice. She said, we must pray on the land. Being in the presence of such a powerful and commanding prayer was reassuring. She then instructed us to start building and the money will come. We immediately called a contractor and gave him all our meager life savings to start the construction. My mom's prayer was fulfilled exactly as stated and within a few months our home was completed.

We stepped out of our comfort zone and decided to take that leap of faith into the unknown with my mother's blessing. This unpredictable journey was exciting, and we embraced each moment joyfully despite the challenges along the way. Once we determined our path, the outcome became possible. We are grateful that we embarked on a journey that led us to live in a mortgage-free home just like my dad did for us growing up.

Stop playing it safe. Stop being scared of being judged by others. Stop feeling that you don't have what it takes because you are not qualified. Stop being afraid of doing the things you want to do. Do not let your purpose and calling pass you by. What is worse than fear is regret—regret that you did not trust God to prepare you for the next level. God is looking for your obedience and trust to allow Him to do what He needs to do in your life and give you the best experience you deserve in this life.

Trust in the LORD with all your heart and lean not on your own understanding.
Proverbs 3: 5

CHAPTER SEVEN

Stepping into Your Comfort Zone

The comfort zone, as defined by Lifehacker, is a "behavioral space where your activities and behaviors fit a routine and pattern that minimizes stress and risk." Typically, our comfort zone is where we are most at home and where we find peace, a sense of familiarity, comfort, certainty and security. Vernon Baker, a black WWII veteran who earned a Purple Heart, stated, "Home is where the heart can laugh without shyness. Home is where the heart's tears can dry at their own pace."

There is nothing wrong with being in your comfort zone as long as it is not permanent and you are fully aware it is a place where you will not experience maximum growth. I was grateful for the opportunity to become comfortable with the security of my husband and the ease of life. Thus far in my journey, I was often unprepared for the challenges of stepping out of my comfort zone, and I would retreat to my comfort zone—a place where I felt grounded. For me, this place is home. Home is a source of special energy for me where I can recharge and regain focus. I feel present and connected with the earth and my beginnings at home. This is where I feel most comfortable and in alignment to take on my goals and purpose.

On my journey, I learned we don't need to be stimulated and challenged in every phase of our life. We need balance, and going to a safe, secure space where you feel accepted is good. As humans, we are creatures of habit and comfort. We enjoy being able to predict our next move and plan for life accordingly. Being in your comfort zone can result in consistent progress to achieve your desired results and goals with little distraction from your pre-set goals.

As I became comfortable in the security and peace of my home in the Dominican Republic, I realized that although I felt safe, I wasn't being challenged intellectually. I felt very small, as if I was shrinking in my environment. I started to question my purpose. As the process becomes routine and monotonous, you must be careful not to get too comfortable holding back and, therefore, not challenge yourself to be creative and grow. I have found that being in my comfort zone for an extended period, I became complacent and began to feel like a hamster's wheel: stagnant, wasted motions with no real goals. The lack of growth made me question my entire existence.

Being uncomfortable, whether or not by choice, can motivate us to accomplish goals we never thought we could. I was motivated to step out of my comfort zone and work as a locums physician. Locum or locus tenens means someone who temporarily fills the duties of another. Although I was stepping into a new position, I was also very comfortable traveling and meeting new people. At this stage, I had lived twice in one US territory, six US states, and one foreign country. So, starting locums, I was surely in my comfort zone, and the other physicians I worked with immediately noticed it.

"Dr. Alexander," they would say, "Why are you so happy?" Most were tired and frustrated with feeling burned out and not valued. Most importantly, they did not feel the support of management and administration. As a locums physician, I did not have the opportunity to feel burned out as most of my contracts lasted anywhere from six to twelve weeks. I rarely dealt with administrators unless they tried to entice me into joining their organization. Being happy in this role was easy. Many physicians do not realize that it isn't your position that makes you happy; it is your disposition. Each day I walked into my job assignment, I would purpose within my heart to be grateful, happy, and cheerful. As King George put it, "The secret to happiness is not doing what one likes but liking what one has to do." And boy, did I love it!

Happiness is something that exists within every one of us. At that stage of my life, I had already grasped the concept of true happiness. Happiness is not found in material or physical things and does not depend on a particular situation or event. Some believe that happiness exists when things are going well, but what happens when a situation takes an opposite turn? Are you no longer happy? My life experiences thus far have taught me that embracing my character strengths, such as humility, gratitude, humor, and perseverance, connects me to the authentic happiness already within me. Be careful of the perception of false or fake happiness because this is where self-doubt, low self-esteem, and the need to have something to sense fulfillment in your life creep in and prevent you from finding your true inner happiness. Happiness may feel different for everyone, but it is a sense of joy and contentment. The Bible lets us know that God wants our joy to be full. As Jesus says in John 15:11, "These things I have spoken to you, that my joy may be in you, and that your joy may be full."

In those halcyon days as a locus tenens physician traveling from one city to the next, the freedom I felt was exhilarating. After working as a locus tenens physician for a couple of years, I decided that the expiration date of days roaming the coast of eastern Florida and sleeping from hotel to hotel was imminent. I felt the need for more stability in my life. Where else would I find such stability but in my comfort zone—the place of familiarity, calmness, safety, and security?

As comforting as this zone is, it is essential to remember not to get too comfortable and hold yourself back instead of challenging yourself to learn and grow. Although I was comfortable practicing as a physician, I was still challenging myself with each new assignment and location. It's also important to remember that you don't have to challenge yourself and be productive constantly. Life is a balance. Retreating to your comfort zone can be essential but also knowing when to leave is also crucial because you don't want to have a negative impact on your life and the world around you by missing any opportunity to display your true purpose and greatness.

After three years as a locums physician, I returned home. The ability to come back home again was a privilege that I did not take for granted. Coming back home to St. Croix, my birthplace, where my navel strings are buried, so to speak, was the ultimate action of stepping into my comfort zone. This was my true home, and I was excited to start a new chapter in my life. This was where I had fond memories of growing up, and I could allow my body and mind to be at ease. This was where I connected with my humble beginnings; the reminders were everywhere. I was quickly reminded of the sense of community and belonging I felt growing up.

Before long, I realized things were not like I remembered, and I found it hard to adjust to what felt like community depression. I was gone for so long that I did not remember many people. I felt like a stranger in my own hometown. I struggled to find a sense of purpose and a fear of not being accepted into the community. Would I even know how to deal with a homogeneous black population as I remembered it as compared to the approximately 98% of Caucasian patients that I typically saw in the clinics on the mainland?

As I settled into my new position, I immediately reconnected with my community and sense of belonging. I knew that returning to the mainland was not an option I desired. I began to appreciate the slower pace of life and found joy in the simple things. I also reconnected with old friends. On one occasion, a particular patient walked in to be seen. In conversation of last names, as was typical in small towns, she realized who my parents were. She informed me she was the best friend of my great-aunt, who had passed away many years prior. As she stared into space, recounting their friendship, she held my hands so I could feel the goosebumps that had risen from her skin, remembering me at six months old, being cared for by my great-aunt—her best friend. She briefly shared one of her favorite pastimes with my great-aunt when they walked long distances daily for exercise. What an emotional experience to sit in front of someone who knew you as an infant, and now you are providing them with healthcare after almost fifty years!

Being terrible with names and faces, I did not recognize her. In usual island life conversations, patients would have realized I was a local physician. She pieced the memories together of many years prior when my sister, my best friend, and I started a cleaning business after college, and she was one of our regular clients. She believed in our business and supported us. Now, here I was, almost twenty years later, sitting in front of her as her doctor. What joy we experienced as she recounted how we taught her to make lasagna. Most incredible was that she remembered the name of our company, Maid Brigade. She had goosebumps as she related the story to me. This is why I came back home. These experiences helped to reconnect shared experiences that helped foster a sense of belonging and my purpose.

While reconnecting with old friends and acquaintances, I made new friends. I began to realize that home is not a place but a feeling. I came back home to find myself, and I succeeded. Home reminded me of my roots where I came from and taught me to be grateful for how far I've come by the grace of God. I saw my home through a new lens and was captivated by its natural beauty, hilly landscapes, and rich, vibrant culture and heritage.

Being away for many years, I did not realize how families can become disconnected as each child pursues their own paths and journeys in different locations. Being back home has reestablished familial bonds and created stronger family connections. My parents have certainly benefitted from the emotional support and companionship.

As for comfort zones, it is good to step out of it, but it's also good to go back in. In your comfort zone, you are more confident in who you are. There is less anxiety and risk, allowing you to draw from past experiences to perform successfully. This creates a positive energy that is mentally stimulating to prepare you for stepping out of your comfort zone at the right time.

Life is a dynamic process and is constantly changing. You are never in the "box" of your comfort zone for too long. While your comfort zone fosters familiarity and calmness, it can also inhibit growth. To make the most of your life, you must learn to balance stepping into and out of your comfort zones with ease and push your limits to achieve your goals while retreating to your familiar space to recharge.

Casting all your cares upon Him,
for he cares for you.
1 Peter 5:7

CHAPTER EIGHT

Keep Moving

Your journey is not only about everything falling into place at the right time but also in the right location. We've all heard the saying, *I was at the right place at the right time.* God has also tied your purpose to your location. Many times in the Bible, we see that when God calls someone on a mission, he calls or sends them to a specific location. When God wanted to bless Abraham, he told him to move to Canaan. Abraham had to leave his country and family to receive the blessing. Joseph had to be relocated to Egypt to fulfill his purpose. Moses had to move to Egypt to fulfill his mission of taking the Israelites out of captivity. In Isaiah 60:22, God states, "At the right time, I, the Lord, will make it happen." So, instead of trying to manipulate your life and worrying about where you are at in life, remember that God will provide for the plan and purpose He created you for.

I learned early in life that to receive my blessings, I had to move. At age seventeen, I had the urge to move away from home, spread my wings, and soar to the location God would use to bless me. Throughout my journey, I have tended to move every three years. Sometimes, it's planned, and other times it's pure happenstance. I studied Medical Technology (Clinical Laboratory Scientist) when I attended undergrad. After three years, I had to enroll in a one-year practicum, allowing me to move to a new location. When I accepted a position at a well-known hospital, which I considered my dream job, I only stayed for three years. I then accepted a locums tenens position and remained on board for three years. I quickly learned that each time I moved, I not only entered a new position where my salary increased, but if I didn't move each time, my life would be completely different.

The one time I did not adhere to my school of thought, I began to feel "stuck." I started to think that my talents, skills, and worth were insignificant. I began to feel small. I shrank in my own reality. The sensation of "feeling stuck" can certainly lead to burnout.

Burnout is a type of stress associated with your job. According to the APA Dictionary of Psychology, burnout is "physical, emotional, or mental exhaustion, accompanied by decreased motivation, lowered performance, and negative attitudes toward oneself and others." Burnout can certainly look different for everyone and can affect individuals emotionally, physically, and mentally. Symptoms can include fatigue, diet or sleep pattern changes, or apathy toward your job.

Once you have identified that you are feeling stuck or burned out, wake up and start planning your next moves, whether that means seeking help for your mental health, lifestyle changes such as exercising, learning new skills, traveling, or receiving that long overdue certification.

In your life, you may also experience relationships that do not appreciate your desire to grow. These situations can drain and suck the life out of you. Surround yourself with others who prioritize you. If it is not possible, be prepared to stay to yourself for a season because you are never alone and this may be your time to connect with God. Growth often requires new relationships, locations, and, most importantly, a new mindset. Once you have created that intention to grow, you will find someone and your tribe who love your drive, encouraging and supporting your every move. If individuals cannot handle your ambitions, they are not meant for you in any way. Your trauma, pain, struggles, or anything that has happened to you does not define you. Your resilience and your trust and faith in God define you. Resilience is your capability to overcome difficult life situations and challenges and still find beauty and connection with a source greater than you—God. God has a purpose for your life. He will release the chains that bind you and remove the feeling of being "stuck." God will turn your trauma, pain, and struggles into purpose.

The quickest way to succeed is to start now. You can surely figure it out as you go along. A wise friend once told me that one should never say you don't have a particular skill when applying for a job. Instead, if you don't have the skill, make it your duty to learn that skill before hire and continue to master the skill upon hire.

I believe motivation is crucial in keeping us in motion. If I want to make it somewhere and become what I want, I use prayer, faith, and discipline as my driving force. So you, too, should stay focused on your course because your moves often will not make sense to others. It is absolutely acceptable if others do not understand your vision. This was the case when a few people discovered I had moved to the Dominican Republic to attend medical school. I am grateful that God used this country to bless me by introducing me to my soulmate.

Upon completing the board exams required to start my medical training, I had a gap where I had to wait for the next application cycle. For me, this certainly did not mean that life would stop at this moment as I waited. I had to keep moving and learning. I was presented with an opportunity to make money while I waited. I saw this opportunity as a means to an end, a way to survive because it did not seem like it had anything to add or complement my goal of becoming a doctor. Little did I know that this opportunity would allow me to grow and trust the process. Being a customer service representative for a satellite radio company represented a new beginning and getting closer to my goal. How could answering the phone pleasantly with a smile on my face while clarifying customers' requests, guiding customers through troubleshooting their satellite radio, or congratulating them on purchasing their satellite radio help me become a better doctor?

I learned the importance of having exceptional customer service skills. It taught me that getting to know my customers went far beyond knowing their names. I had to understand their needs and wants, what problem I would solve for them, what motivated them to use the product, or why they did not like the product or service. These lifelong skills became necessary for every patient I would see and treat as they are also customers. I provide them with my healing and caring service, ensuring they are satisfied. These skills helped me build trust between my patients and myself. If my patients felt they were being treated well by me, they were more likely to comply with their treatment plan and become healthier.

As time goes on, it will not matter how long it takes. As long as you strive for newer heights every day of your life, that is what is important. I certainly learned the importance of God's time. During medical school, there was a rumor that students who started during my time period could have their curriculum reverted to the previous curriculum because of a technicality. I was told the best part was that this would shave off at least a semester or two from the current curriculum. I was so excited about this opportunity and believed in my heart this would be an avenue to finish medical school sooner and save money. I took this information seriously and decided not to take any chances, so I fasted and prayed for an entire weekend. I was on my knees, crying, pleading, and begging God to open this way for me.

Monday morning, I took my friend's advice and spoke to several individuals who I was told would assist me in the process of changing my curriculum. I didn't understand that a process that seemed so simple for others became extremely difficult for me. It didn't matter who I spoke to or who spoke on my behalf; I hit a brick wall every time. I didn't understand why God did not answer my prayer and allowed them to change my curriculum, especially after I fasted and prayed. After tears and frustration, I gave it up. I had to keep moving. I could not let this one obstacle deter me from reaching my goal of completing medical school. I accepted my fate, realizing that I was already in medical school, and if this was the curriculum I needed, then let it be.

Shortly after that, I received the opportunity to do the Kaplan review course provided for the first time at the university. This review course was instrumental in providing the foundation for passing my exams. It wasn't until years later that I realized that if I had graduated sooner, I would not have had the opportunity to do the Kaplan review course, meaning God saw beyond my request and knew what was best. He not only provided the course, but he also placed the most compelling instructor I had ever had to teach the course. For some reason, this instructor believed in me. She made me feel I had absolutely nothing to worry about. She had more confidence in me than I had in myself. I asked her to practice physical examination techniques to prepare for my Step 2 practical exam, which required us to examine actors in a simulated medical setting based on the appropriate history provided. She did not hesitate to be my practice patient. I went through the motions of history taking, asking her the appropriate questions, and then examining her as any physician would. After we practiced several cases, I knew I was ready to tackle the exam. I passed my exams with flying colors and became a doctor, just the way God wanted me to. These life experiences became invaluable life lessons that shaped who I am as an individual. At times, these experiences can be challenging as they can push you to limits that reveals your inner strengths and potential.

God's timing and location are perfect! It is usually not the timing and location we want or expect, but it is certainly what we need. We must trust Him and his plan for our lives because He sees the big picture. Sometimes, God intentionally closes doors because he wants you to keep moving in the direction he places in front of you. This can sometimes be difficult and tough, but you must wait on Him. This does not mean to sit still and do nothing. It conveys more of how you wait. You wait prayerfully, requesting strength and guidance to trust and obey, adapting to His will. This life lesson of adaptability is crucial as it teaches you that the dynamics of going with the flow rather than creating resistance can transform your trials and hardships into opportunities for growth.

In the preparation for your goals, there will be ups and downs. There will be moments when you feel over-whelmed with life and its struggles. The ancient Chinese philosopher Lao Tzu's quote, "Be still like a mountain and flow like a river," is redolent of the Biblical passage of Psalm 27:14, which reminds us to wait on the Lord, be of good courage, and He shall strengthen thine heart. If you have a dream or idea, start working on it. You are not expected to be an expert from the beginning. Each step to your goal is a learning process, which you should embrace wholeheartedly. Make it a point to ground yourself into stillness by scheduling moments with God. This will connect you to the Source of your purpose, and you will receive peace from there. Everything will flow, and trust that everything that needs to be accomplished will be done as you enjoy life in the present. You will see that life will become fulfilling as you stay in constant motion, - learning, growing and connecting.

You are amazing for just getting started. Getting started will tap into your unlimited potential and push you to the next level of excellence. You'll be glad you took a chance on yourself and didn't give up. Do not be afraid to move and position yourself in the right location to seize a once-in-a-lifetime opportunity. You will never know until you make that move. It may just be the best thing you ever did for your life, or maybe not. If it is not, then there's a lesson to learn. Either way, make that move and receive your blessing. Break free from your self-doubts and seek God's will as you walk confidently in His purpose for your life. Keep moving and evolving because each step will bring you closer to your goals, dreams, and purpose. Remember that you don't have to be great to start, but you have to start to be great.

Whatever is true, whatever is noble, whatever is right, whatever is pure, whatever is lovely, whatever is admirable—if anything is excellent or praiseworthy— think about such things.
Phil 4:8

CHAPTER NINE

Positive on Purpose

So you want to live your best life? So, honestly, how do you go about living your best life? How do you make your life worth living and joyful? How do you thrive despite all the challenges that life throws at you? How do you avoid merely existing instead of living a fulfilling life? These are all questions you should address if you feel stuck and don't know why, if life feels unbearable and miserable, or if you just feel lost. The reality is that nothing stays the same. Our needs and wants change over time. Perhaps that dream job or *made-for-each-other* relationship no longer provides you with the stimulation it once did, but you are still afraid of letting go of it.

One way you can start changing your life is to change your mindset. According to Oxford University Press, your mindset is an established set of attitudes of a person or group concerning culture, values, philosophy, frame of mind, outlook, and disposition. The gap between the life you want and the life you're living is determined by your mindset. Mindset also arises from your beliefs about the meaning of life. Your meaning should connect to your purpose. Knowing the purpose of why you are on this Earth is crucial to living a fulfilled and happy life.

Each person's life has its own unique and specific meaning. The greatest challenge in life is discovering who you are. The second greatest is being happy with what you find. This is the belief that you were born to do something—your purpose. Think of purpose as your personal mission statement: The purpose of my life is to share the secrets of how to live your best life. The purpose of my life is to travel the world and share what I've learned about different cultures. The purpose of my life is to show you how to find your divine purpose and live the life of your dreams. The purpose of my life is to spread positivity.

Knowing your purpose and understanding why you were placed on this Earth is vital to living a life of happiness, joy, and fulfillment. It gives you a sense that your life matters. Be intentional about your purpose because it is not what you do for yourself but its impact on others. Your purpose is not your position or job title. It's not awards or achievements. It's not the physical things you are doing. Your purpose is to use your gifts, talents, and opportunities to glorify God in whatever you do and wherever you are. You are not the hero because, without God, you cannot do anything. The significance of human existence is for others to discern value in your actions.

Your primary purpose in life is to bring glory to God. Romans 11:36 says, "For everything comes from Him and exists by His power and is intended for His glory."

Instead of wandering aimlessly through life, connect to your values; you will recognize and understand who you truly are and what you really want. Life can lose meaning when you become disconnected from your values. You become less authentic to yourself and the world around you. Living a purposeful existence where you can discern value in your thoughts, beliefs, and actions is the goal of a meaningful life.

God is with you and will empower you to do what he wants you to do. Invest in things that align with your purpose. Knowing your purpose also lets you prioritize your energy toward flourishing in life. Instead of doing things that make you unhappy or that harm your well-being, you can do things that support your bigger life's purpose. Finding your purpose and higher calling in life is crucial because it gives you a sense of direction. Learn to connect with God to provide you with direction. Discovering your purpose can help you learn how to find your dreams and achieve them. It creates a self-awareness that allows you to make the most of your life.

Try to look at the positive instead of the negative in every situation. As a self-proclaimed optimist, I tend to view the past, present, and future in a positive light. I am not saying you should minimize the negative experience, but focus on boosting your well-being with positivity, engagement, and meaning. Try to restructure your mind to look at situations from a different perspective on purpose; life is not happening to me but *for* me. Do not focus on things that you cannot change. Instead, focus on accomplishments from the past or what challenges you have already overcome. Acknowledging your accomplishments will give you a sense of satisfaction and fulfillment and improve your overall mood. If your path to reaching your goals is more difficult, it is because your calling is HIGHER. Hardships have prepared ordinary people for an extraordinary destiny.

Positive thoughts rewire your brain. Your thoughts are powerful as they can spark emotions that trigger an action that can determine your reality. We all have the capability through our thoughts to influence our future. Resist the desire to interfere with patterns of negative thinking. WATCH YOUR THOUGHTS, and do not let negativity suck the life out of you. Negative thoughts are damaging and can affect your mental health by leading to increased stress, depression, and anxiety. Overall, negative thinking can rob you of your well-being. It can affect your ability to change your life positively and become successful.

Your thoughts can propel you in the direction you need to go, or they can dig you deeper into the miry clay of negativity. If you want to be happy, you have to be happy on purpose. When you wake up, you can't just see what kind of day you'll have; you must decide what kind of day you'll have. For example, start speaking positivity into your life; this will change how you think and speak.

You will notice that your thoughts become words, your words become actions, and your actions become your reality.

Similarly, a negative thought can become a negative reality, and a positive thought can become a positive reality. If you want to be positive, you have to be positive on purpose. Surround yourself with positivity. Being positive does not mean ignoring the negative but rather overcoming the negative. When bad things happen, you focus on the positive and keep going rather than focusing on the bad. The stamina to keep going through your struggles with positivity and optimism is truly the definition of resilience. Life is full of challenges, setbacks, and surprises. Resilience does not make you immune to them. Resilience allows you to bounce back and learn from them and is vital to improving self-discipline. Without denying the reality of any adverse situation, positive thinking is another tool in your arsenal for when adversity strikes. Your thoughts can harness your God-given power.

Life's ultimate goal should be to impact the world around you positively. Even if you cannot directly help someone, you should still strive to avoid causing harm. This emphasizes that we are all connected and that our actions can either lift or bring others down. The single most important predictor of happiness is social connections. Connections with others can promote positive mental and physical health, provide support and joy, decrease anxiety and depression while teaching us about trust, empathy and cooperative relationships. Throughout my life experiences, I have learned to trust my inner strength and resilience and lean on others. The beauty of life comes from genuine human connections. We connect with others by opening up and sharing who we genuinely are and in turn experience, tangible and emotional support, gratitude, and positive emotions.

As a physician, I am grateful for opportunities that present themselves daily for me to connect with others. I recall one patient who informed me he had treated his urinary tract infection with a particular plant. I asked him to bring the plant to the clinic at his earliest convenience. Immediately after his visit, he proudly brought several plants and educated me on the names and uses of each plant. Through sheer curiosity and being fully engaged in his presentation, we were able to stretch our intelligence and emotional capacity while appreciating his skill. He in turn was grateful for my willingness to engage with him and he accepted the prescription I provided for his infection.

I also make it a habit to intentionally engage with my patients over 85 years of age and asked them to share words of wisdom after each visit. I experienced a deeper connection and interest when the octogenarians shared advice: Don't believe everything you read in the newspaper or hear on television. Never buy a Mercedes. Stay natural. Drink lots of water. Drink bush tea. Rest. Exercise. Don't have children and trust God, to name a few. Because of these simple yet engaging conversations, I came away from the visits feeling as if I truly connected with my patients and was open to appreciating different perspectives and shared wisdom.

Human connection is the fabric of our being, and micro-moments of interactions are just as authentic. Your ability to flourish as a human being depends on your ability to experience positive emotions, such as love, happiness, enjoyment, contentment, satisfaction, and affection. There's healing in positivity. You have the capacity to choose life, to choose health, and to choose love! You should try to connect with others every day, no matter what, as this will not only improve your well-being but also theirs.

Another simple way to cultivate positive thinking is through gratitude. Be grateful for your unique journey—the highs, the lows, the blessings, the lessons, the setbacks, and the comebacks. Your life is unique journey filled with experiences that teaches you about your fears, failures, growth, challenges, resilience and love. Say thank you to the boss who overlooked you multiple times for a promotion even though you met all the qualifications. Thank you for the criticism that likely made you doubt your capabilities and question God. Through sincere prayer, you became grateful that God knew best all along. You realized God wanted you to have the desire to elevate yourself because they refused you. You also learned that God will not put His children in a toxic environment. You are His child and deserve so much more respect.

So, no matter what happens, be confident and have faith in God's plan so that you don't even get upset when things don't go your way because someday, you will truly be grateful that God gave you what you needed instead of what you thought you wanted. Gratitude is not a brain state, but it is crucial as it allows people to appreciate and enjoy what is good. Be grateful for everything and make the best of it. Your gratitude will be your secret to happiness. Happiness is the meaning and purpose of life.

God wants us to live our best life. He wants us to be happy. John 10:10, the New Living Translation, says, "My purpose is to give them a rich and satisfying life." You can manifest the good life by realizing that you are God's handiwork, accepting His plan for you, living right, praying for others, and obeying God's commands. God has it all planned out for you, but you have to do your part and make the right choices. Living the good life is a courageous journey, a gradual acknowledgment and realization of the possibilities God has placed before you as you fulfill your calling in God's Kingdom. Live purposefully, chase what brings you joy, live in the moment, find gratitude in the small things, and set boundaries to protect your peace.

Never Give Up + Stay Positive + Do Your Best = Success
Love Yourself + Love What You Do + Love How You Live
= Happiness

"For I know the plans I have for you," declares the Lord, "plans to prosper you and not to harm you, plans to give you hope and a future."
Jeremiah 29:11

CHAPTER TEN

Dare to Dream

My life has been anything but linear and definitely defies societal molds. God had a plan for my life before I had a plan for myself, and He orchestrated every detail. Whenever I decided to make my own plans without God, He showed me that my plan had to fail for His to prevail, like the time when I applied to hundreds of US medical schools, only for God to allow each one of them to reject me for Him to take me to a foreign country to learn another language, graduate from medical school, and marry my soulmate.

Stop letting your fears get in the way of experiencing a full and tantalizing life. This does not mean you should be irresponsible and dangerous, but open your mind to thrive in what brings you happiness and joy. Instead of worrying about what others might think of you, enjoy and be present in every moment like your life depended on it. Make a big deal about the simple things such as going for a walk, getting ice cream, riding a bike, reading, listening to music, or even washing your hair. Stop depending on a false sense of security like that job you hate going to every day, that relationship that doesn't excite you anymore, or friendships you know are not right for you. Ask yourself this: if your situation does not change, can you live out your heart's desire? If not, make a plan to change it.

When I look back on my life, there was no delay, closed door, or rejection that God didn't eventually use for my good. Also, while looking back at my journey, I realized everything happened the way it was meant to be and was worth it. After many disappointments became blessings, I began to understand the pattern. If everything I ever hoped and dreamed for came easy, I wouldn't be the person I am today.

Never give up on your dream because you think it will take too long to accomplish. Your dreams are God-given, and He placed them within you to give you a sense of purpose. Following your dream is to make a decision based on faith and not fear. You should believe in your purpose so strongly that others can't help but believe in you, too. You may get discouraged when you focus on the destination. The time will pass. It doesn't matter how long it takes to get there because it will require time and effort. Without discipline, dreams are just dreams; when you accept hard work, your wildest dreams can come true. Once you accomplish it, you'll be glad you took a chance on yourself and didn't give up.

Sometimes, God takes you on a journey you didn't know that you needed to give you everything you desire.

Throughout my struggles and challenges, I eventually learned I didn't become angry or upset when things did not go my way. Instead, I became excited to see what God had in store for me. You should allow your natural essence to flow, whether the waves are rough or calm. It's important to stay calm and focus during the hardships. You should not worry about what you can't see on the horizon.

Once again, how can I forget the words written across my seventh-grade classroom wall? *"Whatever the mind can conceive and believe, it can achieve"* (Napoleon Hill) has manifested in my life. Everything is possible: your dreams, your ideas, your vision. Never let anyone tell you, "You can't." Don't let anyone take you for granted. Know when you deserve better, and don't be afraid to move on. Trust that the same God who got you where you are will get you out of anything that is not right for you. Have faith even when you don't understand why or see the end. I was told, "Your MCAT score isn't good. You won't get into medical school. You can't apply to medical school because you had a C in organic chemistry." Yet, I overcame everything. Now, here I am, doing all these things and more. Don't let anyone tell you that you are not good enough. Instead, let their expectation be the fuel for your goals. Listen to your heart and follow your dream because you are more powerful than you can imagine. You have a purpose, and God loves you.

At the beginning of 2022, a little over one year after my father-in-law passed from COVID-19, my husband was diagnosed with COVID-19. Being away from him, I tried to encourage him to stay hydrated, but the COVID-19-related vomiting and diarrhea were too much for him to bear alone. The comfort and soups of friends did not give him the strength to fight the respiratory syndrome. He knew it was getting too serious to remain at home when he began having shortness of breath and difficulty climbing the stairs to the second floor.

I immediately informed my job that I had to leave. I saw my last patient and packed my bags for the airport. I wanted to be there to protect him and make sure that I was there when the doctors treated him. He also wanted to wait for my arrival before going to the hospital. In God's style and fashion, my flight was delayed several times, and it was close to midnight. We knew my husband could no longer wait for my arrival and would have to check in to the hospital before his condition worsened. Reluctantly, he presented to the emergency department and was diagnosed with bilateral COVID-19 pneumonia. He was immediately admitted to the ICU, where patients were stripped of all their personal belongings, including their cell phones, cutting off all communication with the outside world. Communication with his friend, who drove him to the hospital, was futile as he was left outside of the emergency department and waited for the arrival of my flight.

During my flight, I experienced many emotions, most of all fear. I was afraid to lose the love of my life, my life partner, and my person. Then, a call came in before boarding my flight, and I recognized the number. It was my husband in a whisper, letting me know that he was in the ICU and he wanted to get out. I was relieved that he felt strong enough to want to leave but terrified that maybe he was being kept against his will. He said he couldn't stay on the phone for long because he sneaked it in and didn't want to get caught. This was the Peter I knew—the fighter.

I encouraged him to remain strong and reminded him I was coming. We hung up after voicing our love for each other. My relief was short-lived when I received another call from a trusted confidant who claimed they had entered the hospital and that my husband was placed on the ventilator. *"Oh no!"* I thought. I just spoke to him, and he sounded fine. It was time to take off, and I had to hang up the phone. I cried the entire flight. My arrival was also futile at 1 a.m. There weren't any doctors to speak to at that time and no one to provide any updates on my husband.

Our friend suggested he take me home to get some rest and return the following day. I felt so helpless. I came all this way and had to leave him alone. Reluctantly, I agreed, knowing that I couldn't sleep. I spent the night crying and praying for his recovery. The prayer warriors, including family, friends, and even social media, were on full deck. We needed all the prayers because I knew I couldn't do it without their support. Then, another phone call came in the early morning hours, and it was Peter. He was okay. He reassured me that he was not on the ventilator. It was not true. The relief I felt was indescribable. I told him how happy I was to hear from him and what I heard. Once again, he reiterated that he needed to get out of there.

The following days were filled with brief videos of him exercising and short calls to prevent his phone from being confiscated. On day three, he stated they would let him go because his follow-up scans did not show any signs of pneumonia. The Infectious Disease physician, who had not seen someone recover so quickly from his pneumonia, was reluctant to release him but also had no reason to keep someone in the ICU who was doing push-ups and jogging in place. It was indeed a miracle for which we praised God. This is a reminder that your faith in God will keep you going, trusting in the plan, and ultimately giving Him all the glory.

God reveals his purpose to you by instilling your dream within you. We all have dreams, hopes and aspirations but we have no clue about the experiences we will go through to accomplish our dream. God will intentionally not show you how to get there. In order for you to achieve your dream, you must become more than you are currently. You must let go of being in control and your fears to experience the desired growth. In order to grow, God must develop your character, personality, mindset, principles and talents through hardships and challenges. It's all part of the process and does not have to make sense to you or others. Between where you are and the end is the plan. Have you noticed that no matter how much you plan, you will never be able to predict the experiences during the process. The plan is to prepare you for your purpose. If God revealed the plan to you including a vision of the hardships and struggle you would have to endure, you would say forget the dream. I had a dream of becoming a doctor, which God placed within me. If I knew everything I would go through to become a doctor, I likely would have told God that this was not for me. If God has revealed to me that from the inception to the completion of writing this book would take ten years mostly filled with self-doubts, I would have likely felt it was a waste of time. Like Joseph in the Bible, where you are may not be where you want to be, but it's part of the plan because no matter your circumstances, God will accomplish His purpose in your life at the right time if you allow Him to.

Your life experiences will help you create the life you want for yourself. We never thought we would be where we are. *"And where are we?"* you might ask. My husband and I have been in a long-distance marriage for most of your marriage. We have been married for many years in a marriage that has experienced its ups and downs. Somehow, the distance has made us closer. It's not because we make time to talk on the phone daily, video chat, and send frequent text messages throughout the day. It's because, most importantly, we put God first in our marriage and fully understand that it was part of the plan.

When we pray, it's for wisdom to make the right decisions, increase connection to each other when we are apart, and for our love to keep growing every day. The only thing that hasn't changed is the heartbreaking emotion we experience saying goodbye to each other. Each time I prepare to board a plane, we share a brief moment of intense sadness as we customarily kiss, and then Peter kisses my forehead as we separate, hoping to see each other again soon. Still, to this day, I get excited and jittery when it's time to visit my husband.

We have overcome the distance, financial struggles, health scares, family abandonment, and many circumstances life threw at us. Through these struggles, we gained the willpower and courage to rise above our difficulties and have the life we dreamed of. We have learned to cherish the times we share—good and bad—and realize that we were made for each other and are truly grateful that God brought us together. This gratitude has sustained us throughout the years. We are best friends. We keep God first and center in our relationship. We have careers that bring us joy and fulfill our purpose. Together, we have accomplished and overcome many obstacles, including building our dream home without a mortgage and frequently traveling to destinations of our dreams. We express our gratitude regularly.

On a trip to Santorini, my husband and I became captivated by its resplendent scenery. At dinner, overlooking the spectacular sunset of Santorini, we began to reminisce about how far we had come to be able to afford and travel to countries that we had only dreamt about. We talked about living in our two-bedroom apartment and how I spent countless hours studying, how he would go off to work, barely making ends meet, and how we would call family members and friends for financial help and be grateful for the twenty or fifty dollars we would receive. With water rolling down our faces, glistening in the reflection of the sunset rays, we felt an abundance of gratitude as we wiped our tears and toasted to a happy life worth living with no regrets of God's plan.

My husband became the perfect piece of my puzzle. I cannot imagine my life without him. Being married to Peter has helped me become who I am. We fit so perfectly together. Not because we are perfect but because we have built each other up to become the best version of ourselves. Our relationship has been strengthened by the struggles we have faced and overcome together. We do not like to be defined by our struggles. Instead, we choose to remember how far we've come and how much we've grown. The power of our marriage has created two individuals perfect for each other, building our lives, goals, and dreams together because we chose to put God first in our marriage as a team. God is bigger and greater than us, and His role in our lives truly sustains us. It is imperative that you choose a partner who is part of the plan. Your partner will be good for you emotionally, spiritually, physically and financially.

My life experiences - being teased for my heritage, cleaning toilets in undergraduate college, signing out books in a library to patrons, processing specimens in a clinical laboratory, and answering phone calls from irate customers in a call center after graduating from medical school, marrying my husband - all provide the framework of a lifetime commitment to my own spiritual and personal development. In these various positions, the statement that people may not always remember what you say, but they will remember the way you made them feel became a reality in my daily activities. It motivated me always to give my best when relating to others, regardless of the walk of life they came from. It also showed that all the hard work and all the struggles eventually paid off.

We have realized that having lots of money, driving fancy cars, and holding fancy job titles are not life's ultimate goals. Of course, money is good and essential, but we choose to value our time, family, relationship with God, and freedom above everything else.

Your lifestyle is your destiny. You practice who you will become every day. If you want to empower others, practice being positive. If you want a fit body, consistently follow your exercise routine and healthy diet. If you want a calm mind, practice meditation. If you want to be happy, practice being grateful and finding joy in the simple things. If you want to be successful, practice being disciplined and focused on your goals. If you want to be spiritual, practice connecting with God. If you want to live the life of your dreams, experience contentment with the past, happiness in the present, and hope for the future.

Health and wellness writer Brad Stulberg states practice is "approaching things that matter deliberately, with presence, and with the intention to improve and grow." We can choose to repeat actions until we become proficient. Consistency and showing up regularly can help lead you to success. Live a life that will create the future you want. When you take responsibility for your thoughts and actions, your outcome will be unstoppable.

You have the power to change your life and start making choices that will lead you to a better future and become who you want to be and not what you want others to see. Knowing your purpose and why you were placed on this earth is vital to living a life of fulfillment and happiness. Your happiness comes from within and not from anyone or the material things around you. Being genuinely grateful and content is the foundation of happiness.

Success is more than achieving your goals. It is living your values and creating the life you want to live. One of the best definitions of success I have encountered is from Maya Angelou, who stated, "Success is liking yourself, liking what you do, and liking how you do it." Let nothing stand between you and the life you want to be living. Design a life that feels good on the inside and not just looks good on the outside. You can design your tomorrow according to what you dream of today. The decisions you make today will change your lifestyle and, ultimately, your future. Nothing you have experienced goes to waste on life's journey; both good and bad experiences shape your mind and heart for what is coming.

Success does not come alone, and I owe who I am to my immediate and extended family and friends. Growing up, I realized it is crucial to pray for others. Amid the stress, worry, disaster, and sickness, prayer has delivered peace, comfort, and rest from my troubles. With prayer, you can release joy through all your hardships. You must never forget, when facing difficulty, to stop in your tracks and pray. This legacy of prayer has prepared me for life and has made me an overcomer.

As you travel to new heights emotionally, spiritually, and physically, it is the moment of truth to rise to the occasion. Your best life will be a reality when you allow God to do His will and for Him to be glorified. The best things happen in God's timing. Whatever your future holds, do not be afraid of the path that appears to be more complicated, as this path will probably produce more failures and struggles that will develop you and give you a life with more meaning. Don't give up, but continue to be grateful for the victories God has brought you through to achieve your purpose. God is responsible for every good thing in my life, and I give him all the glory and praise for everything. Life will not be perfect, but there are several essential factors that you should know. This will encourage you along your journey of learning and growing.

1. God wants you to have a good life.
2. You should follow God's will.
3. Watch how you speak.
4. Be ready to sacrifice.

5. Pray for others.

6. Have integrity.

7. Be joyful.

When God has something for you, it doesn't matter who stands in the way. He will move whatever obstacle is in your way to get you through. He states in Jeremiah 29:11, "For I know the plans I have for you … plans to prosper you and not to harm you, plans to give you hope and a future." In Isaiah 60:22, God also reminds you that he will make it happen at the right time. God will provide for the plan and purpose He created you for. Do not worry. Instead, find peace, knowing what is for you will be for you.

You were meant for greatness. Greatness isn't about your actions but also your restraints. Jesus defined greatness as serving others for His glory. He measures greatness in terms of service, not status. You should refrain from putting yourself first but be humble, never feeling that you are above or better than anyone as you fulfill your purpose. Never let anyone extinguish the effervescent flame that fuels your purpose. I admonish you to go confidently toward your dreams for a rich, satisfying life full of joy. Decide today to make the rest of your life the best of your life. Find yourself a supportive group of people who will inspire you to live to your fullest potential and hold you accountable for accomplishing your dreams. Living your best life is a journey that takes you on the path and possibilities that God has in store for you as you fulfill your purpose.

The strength of a woman is not measured by the impact that all her hardships in life have had on her; but the strength of a woman is measured by the extent of her refusal to allow those hardships to dictate her and who she becomes.

C. JoyBell C.

Endnotes

I am so grateful for those who have cheered me along the way and provided valuable resources through their support, encouragement, thoughts, and advice—people like Ramone Reid, Johanne Joseph, and Rodney Kidd, JD. You have no idea how you have inspired me and how those conversations connected with me and gave me the spark to *just do it*! Thank you from the bottom of my heart for not accepting me just as I am but pushing me toward my full potential.

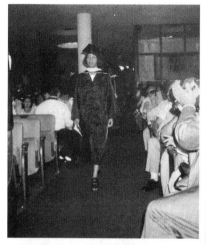

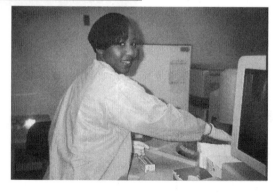

About The Author

D r. Annetta Alexander, a native of St. Croix US Virgin Islands graduated from the St. Croix Seventh-day Adventist School. She completed her Bachelor's of Science in Medical Technology at CUC now known as Washington Adventist University. Dr. Alexander went on to complete her Master of Public Health from Virginia Commonwealth University and her medical degree from the Universidad Central del Este in the Dominican Republic. She completed her Internal Medicine and Pediatrics internship and residency at East Carolina University in North Carolina. Dr. Alexander currently practices in St. Croix, USVI.

Dr. Alexander is married to Dr. Peters Jean Noel. In her spare time, she enjoys traveling, spending time with family, spending time outdoors, reading, volunteering and learning languages. She is fluent in Spanish, French based Creoles and currently learning Arabic. She has been involved in medical missions in the Dominican Republic, Haiti and Ghana. She was named among Top Internist in Florida for several years and received the Patient's Choice Award.

Made in the USA
Columbia, SC
10 November 2024

45904272R00076